Parenting a Strong-Willed Child

How to Effectively Raise High Spirited Children or Toddlers

By: Discover Press

Table of Contents

Preface

Bang, bang, bang!

I remember the pain like it was yesterday.

Bang, bang, bang!

I sat on the edge of the bed, clutching the video baby monitor in one hand and my wife's hand in the other, as we watched our two-year-old son throw a gigantic tantrum on the floor of his room. It was well past bedtime, but he decided that 7:30 PM was way too early to go to bed. Instead, he chose to lay on the floor and stomp his feet against the door for two hours straight.

Bang, bang, bang!

My wife looked at me with tears in her eyes. "How long do we let him go on like this?" I shook my head and shrugged, as if to say, "I do not know."

Initially, we tried to go in at certain intervals. Every five to ten minutes, one of us would walk in, gently close the door behind us, and soothe our child until we were convinced he would drift off to sleep in our arms. But every single time, as soon as we closed the door behind us, we heard the scampering of feet, which then turned into stomping on the door as he screamed for us to let him out.

And before you ask, we even tried leaving the door open. That didn't work either, because as soon as we left the room on those occasions, he would follow us out to our own bedroom. Every. Single. Time.

Bang, bang, bang!

Eventually, it was up to me. My wife was hormonal at the time, so every shriek and cry coming from my son's room sent her into overdrive. In reality, I was trying to sooth two people: my two-year-old son, and my pregnant wife.

Did I forget to mention that? That my wife was pregnant at the time with our second child? That threw a whole new wrench in the equation, not just because of the hormones, but also because of the sinking feeling you get in the pit of your stomach when you begin to believe that if you cannot take care of one child, how in the world can you take care of two?

I had read nearly every book I could get my hands on in the nine months leading up to my son's birth, but nothing prepared me for the reality of overnight feedings, constant diaper changes, and the protective feeling that dominated every second of every day. Eventually, you simply begin to wear out—both mentally and physically—until you find yourself perfectly content to stare into the wall just to get a little peace.

Not that there hadn't been good times; on the contrary, the last two years had been nothing short of magical. Absolutely nothing in this world beats the experience of holding your child in your own arms, knowing that they will always look to you for guidance, encouragement, and at times, a little bit of discipline. You are their protector, their friend, their mentor, and their rock. As a parent, you alone bear that responsibility. As a parent, it is up to you to figure it out.

Bang, bang, bang!

I don't remember what time he fell asleep that night, but I do know that I woke up the next morning on the floor of his room, with him nestled in his bed, sound asleep. I rolled over onto my elbow and stared at my son, wondering how in the world I could've been so scared of a little child. I stroked his hair, and put my hand on his stomach as I felt his breath go in and out. It was a nervous habit that I had developed very early in his little life—just my way of telling myself that he was okay.

I crawled across the floor and stumbled into the kitchen where I discovered, thankfully, that I had set the coffee for the next morning. I poured myself a cup, and then turned around and noticed my wife waddling in with her enormous, pregnant belly. She did not even ask - she just grabbed the cup from my hands and walked to the couch.

"How are we supposed to do it, Steve?" she asked. "If it is this bad with one kid, how are we supposed to handle a second?"

I stroked my wife's hand. "One day at a time."

****

Nearly fifteen years have passed since that night on the floor of Eric's room, and still I remember that pain. I remember the frustration of looking at my child and not knowing how in the world I was supposed to not only keep him safe, but also turn him into a fully functioning adult. Interestingly enough, we went on to have three more children, none of whom gave us nearly as much of a fight as Eric did day in and day out. And yet, I wouldn't trade any of those difficult years for anything. They helped shape Eric.

Still, I meet parents every single week that come to me with tears in their eyes, saying that they have no idea how they are supposed to help their child. They say things like:

"Nothing works. We have tried everything we can think of, but there is just no getting through to him."

Or, "The therapist says she's just a tough kid. We just have to grin and bear it, knowing that her stubbornness will pay off down the road."

Or possibly the hardest one. "I do not know what to do. I'm really worried about him."

I can sympathize with all these statements—as a parent, and as a writer. I know what it feels like to be in their shoes, feeling deflated and beaten down, worried about the future of someone you love so much.

That is why I wanted to write this book. More than anything else, what I want to tell you—you, the parent of a child that is so strong-willed that every day feels like a Battle Royale—that everything is going to be okay.

Breathe.

Relax.

It is going to be fine.

I'm happy to report that today, Eric is a thriving 17-year-old high school student. He's got a job, good grades, healthy relationships, and a bright future that my wife and I are both very excited about. And as much as I'd love to say that it directly results from our amazing parenting, the reality is that he is a good kid. As tough as he was—and still is, in so many ways—those attributes have helped create a life for him.

I could not be prouder, and I would go through all those sleep-on-the-floor nights again a hundred times over if I knew that this is how it would work out.

That is why I wanted to tell you this again. As hard as it is now, everything is going to be okay.

Do you believe me?

If not, that is fine. The only thing I ask is that you give me a chance to explain how everything is going to be okay.

I know it doesn't feel like it now, but your child's stubbornness is going to pay off with dividends down the road. Think of your child not as a powder keg ready to explode, but a piece of marble that you, as a master craftsman, must chisel away at, piece by piece.

It will not be easy, but then again, what parent would honestly admit that any kid ever is? They all have their difficulties—no matter if it is stubbornness or its equally dangerous cousin, apathy—so do not fall into the trap of feeling like your child is "broken" in some way.

And please, for the sake of your sanity, do not start comparing little Junior to the neighbor kid down the street. I guarantee you they are fighting their own battles behind closed doors that you know nothing about. Making a decision about your own child based on limited information of someone else's is unfair—to yourself, and to your child. Don't do it. Just don't.

Within these pages, I try to distill my own expertise in working with parents into a several short, easy-to-read chapters. I do not want this to read as a dry, academic text; instead, I'd rather the following pages feel like a conversation with a trusted friend. Imagine that you called me to vent about your children, and we got together for coffee to talk through some things. I'm not the "expert" in that sense—just a compassionate ear.

It is my goal, however, that you will find strength through these pages—strength that you are not alone, and strength to simply get through another day.

I guarantee you, it is worth it.

Chapter 1: Identifying the Strong-Willed Child

Putting a label on any kid is dangerous.

I see parents all the time who insist that their kid is "smart," "dedicated," or—my personal favorite—"very advanced for their age." While invariably, some of these may turn out to be true, I have found that many of the parents that I talk to grossly miscalculate who and what their child is.

By the same token, some parents think that their kids are the absolute worst; and while they would never admit that to their child in-person, within the confines of a cozy office where everything can be explored openly, they relay to me their concerns about their children. Some say that their kids are troublemakers, or that they fear deeply for their kids' futures. Others label them while they are still way too young; one parent, in particular, told me that her son was "slow academically." The kid was in first grade.

There are a billion reasons for this misperception, the first one being that we are too emotionally attached to our kids in order to give a fair evaluation. We either have high dreams for them—which are inevitably shattered—or we remember a few minor hiccups throughout the day and extrapolate that on a global scale. A child that cannot color inside the lines, for instance, does not understand authority, according to the parents. In reality, one hardly ever equals the other.

As parents, what we need to do is zoom out and view our children through an objective lens. What I'm not suggesting is that you take a clipboard and a checklist and mark off every single behavior as positive or negative, but I would ask you to examine your child honestly. Are they actually rebellious, or do you just have too restrictive rules? Are they actually overachieving, or do you just underestimate your child? Bedtimes and mealtimes are two of the most common flashpoints for parents, so if your child resists the most at these two times, how different are they, really?

The goal here is to find commonalities between how your children behave and how a child at their age is supposed to behave, so that you can establish a baseline for their behavior. Once you have done that, you can analyze the progress that is made over the course of the next six to twelve months and see whether or not they are progressing at an age-appropriate level.

Sounds simple, right?

By and large, however, I almost never put labels on a child unless multiple indicators point to the most reasonable solution, or if ignoring the signs would cause damage to the child somehow—emotionally, intellectually, or physically. A child that is dyslexic cannot simply be marked off as having a learning disability; you must give them the tools to thrive, or else they will stay behind forever and resent you in the process.

Identifying the strong-willed child comes with similar pitfalls, but it also comes with the same necessities. By using very common markers, we can form a reasonable basis about a child based on their current behavior and project where they will be several years from now. While there is no hard and fast "pass/fail" metric, if your child has the majority of these traits, it is worth talking to somebody that can understand your child's specific situation more clearly.

Restlessness

Continuing a point made earlier, all kids are restless to some degree. Trying to keep a child silent and still during a religious service, as many parents know, is a miracle in and of itself. Many parents tell me that they have not been able to worship effectively in years because they have been too busy trying to keep all their kids quiet during an hour-long service.

Strong-willed children do everything fast. They want to go now, they want to eat now, they want to leave now, and they do not want to wait a second longer or else they will start being vocal about their irritation. So, while mild restlessness is not usually a problem, and is remarkably common amongst most kids, having a child that throws a fit a few seconds after being told to wait can be a strong indication that your child has an unbreakable will that is all their own.

Demanding

Have you ever tried to please a toddler? I cannot tell you how many times I have sat in the McDonald's drive-through line and asked my kids whether they wanted a hamburger or chicken nuggets at the window, only to have one's mind change four different times in fifteen seconds, resulting in that child eventually getting a fish-filet meal instead (still not sure how that happened).

Regardless, some children take it up a notch. Instead of just trying to play older people like a puppet, others are demanding, exerting their will over other human beings to force them to act the way that they want them to act. It is not just about having an opinion that needs to be heard—they have a distinct preference as to how certain things should be done, and anything done differently is just a travesty.

Independent

Who does not want to raise an independent child? Ideally, all kids will grow under the parent's watchful eye, only to flourish once they arrive in the world on their own.

But while independence is praised, a child that refuses to obey any kind of instructions—whether by a parent, teacher, or someone else—is a child that will require a more diligent eye to train. This is not necessarily bad; in fact, these happy kids generally prefer to learn on their own rather than by following a script. Nevertheless, you cannot break the rules until you know the rules, and getting a child to follow certain guidelines in the first place can sometimes be the most challenging part.

Stubborn

Ask anyone who has kids, and they will tell you that one of the most difficult parts of raising a child is getting them to follow what you tell them to do. No matter if it is eating vegetables or brushing their teeth, most children need to be told two or three times to perform even the most basic tasks. But if your child knows exactly what needs to be done and simply refuses to do it, it can be a sign that you are not just dealing with an average toddler, but a strong-willed child that will require more creative ways to get the message across.

Opinionated

All kids have opinions, but strong-willed kids will defend theirs far longer than others do. No matter if they initially agreed to whatever it was you asked them to do in the first place, their attitude can change on a dime, and then you will be dealing with a kid who more closely resembles a stone wall. Even if you can engage them in conversation, they will most likely talk back, pleading their case as to why their way is better a hundred times out of a hundred.

If they do decide to go along with your line of reasoning, they will inevitably want to know why. Nothing is less satisfactory to them than hearing the phrase "because I said so," because that does not resonate with them. A child that is bent on refuting any kind of authority figure inside their life is not going to acknowledge your own authority unless it is qualified by something else. What exactly? Usually their own opinion.

Prone to Tantrums

Few things are more frustrating for a parent than when a child has a complete meltdown, especially if that meltdown happens in a very public place such as a grocery store or a restaurant. But if you are the parent of a strong-willed child, you should be prepared for this to happen on a much more frequent basis. Since many of them do not have the capabilities of reasoning through their own case and working around an issue, they will resort to screaming and possibly even violence. These fits can come on suddenly and fiercely, usually manifesting in a matter of seconds.

As a parent, one of the hardest parts of this entire episode may be the inability to understand what is setting the child off in the first place. In some situations, it may be something obvious, such as someone who refuses to eat their vegetables. At other times, you may simply be walking down the toy aisle, and passing by a child's favorite toy too quickly could send them into orbit. Regardless, the best thing you can do in this situation is acknowledge the feelings of your child; dismissing them out of hand will only make it worse.

Moral Compass

You may think that kids do not develop a sense of right and wrong till much later in life, but recent research suggests that kids begin to understand the difference between right and wrong around nineteen months of age. Most children will have their moral compass crafted by the parent or guardian, allowing their minds to be molded by whatever their authority figures fashion in their life.

Not so with strong-willed children. Many of them have made their mind up as to what the right course of action is long before they are informed—at least intentionally—by a parent, and will fight to the death to defend their position. There is very little persuasion that a parent can do to help a situation like this; and indeed, too many rules will overwhelm the child and cause them to fight for every single thing. Pick your battles, and do not be afraid to let the minor ones slide.

Argue

In case the previous guidelines do not cover it, a strong-willed child loves few things more than arguing. Most of the time, the argument is not even about the issue at hand; instead, it is a Battle Royale for sheer dominance. They do not care what they win, as long as they win.

One of the hallmarks for strong-willed children is their ability to find every single weakness in your argument. They are experts at bringing things up that you've long since forgotten, such as the caveat you gave three weeks ago about getting dessert after dinner as long as they finished what is required first. Today, they will demand that you give them the treat because of the same logic that you used in the past.

15

If any of the above traits sound familiar, then you most likely have a strong-willed child under your roof. While all kids will have some, or even all, of these traits to a certain degree, the key is finding these to an extreme level. In other words, if your child sees that fighting in and of itself is the end goal, then you may be in for a tough time. But are they really just combative, or is there something deeper happening? That is what we'll discuss in the next chapter.

Chapter 2: Is Your Child Strong-Willed...or Just Rebellious?

Often, in my dealings with parents, the real question is not what to do about the immediate behavior that is taking place, but whether or not that behavior will ultimately lead to developmental issues down the road. Those are valid concerns, and ones that I always try to tackle on a case-by-case basis as objectively as I can.

There is good news and bad news. The bad news is that recent studies have suggested there is a link to a child's early development issues and problems that may develop down the road. Questions with authority now may lead to questions with authority later—in some cases, even aggressively. These traits tend to manifest themselves between the ages of three and twelve, just as a child is learning to cope with boundaries that are placed on them by others.

The good news is that there also seems to be evidence suggesting that temperament and parenting are linked more than we ever knew before, especially regarding strong-willed children. A child that is more easy-going, for example, will not be as impacted by parenting practices as one who is strong-willed, meaning that you have the ability to create a greater impact on your child than others.

Or, to put it even more simply, no child's temperament is set in stone.

The absolute worst thing that any parent can do is to simply throw their hands up in the air and give up on their child completely. While no parent will ever consciously make such a decision, I have seen many parents that try to rationalize their child's behavior by saying things like, "That is just the way they are," or "I have tried everything, and nothing works. I guess we are just stuck like this."

If that is the way you are thinking about your child, then the first thing you need to do is automatically cease and desist that type of mindset. Contrary to popular opinion, a strong-willed child craves greater interaction with their parents and with others. The only thing you have to do is help them navigate it.

I have also seen parents that blame themselves for their children's mistakes. When the kid is not in the room, there is a very heavy sense of self-loathing, often resulting in parents bringing up events that happened years in the past, almost seeing their child's present behavior as some kind of atonement for previous transgressions. Not only is that mindset not helpful, it is also extremely destructive to the relationship.

Strong-willed children require strong-willed parents. That does not mean you must lash out at your child every single time there is an issue at stake, but you do have to be tough enough to handle some serious mudslinging in the early years in the hopes that you are molding a future warrior. Even if their behavior becomes worse, you shouldn't look at it as a failure, but as progress toward the end goal. As long as they are communicating with you, they are moving in the right direction.

Along those lines, allow me to take a step back and give you a word of encouragement. Any parent can handle an easy-going child. One who is agreeable, quiet, and friendly is every parent's dream. What takes guts is taking a child that most people would struggle with and making them a multiyear project. Make no mistake about it, parent, you are in the fight of your life, but it is not a matter of good versus evil or even you versus them; it is about the present and the future. You are exchanging short-term pain for long-term stability, enthusiasm, and independence. Those are the traits that every parent truly wants out of their child, regardless of what they are like when they are five.

Rebellion is different from a strong-willed nature in several ways. The biggest one is that a rebellious child is actively feeding on the parent's lack of consistency. If a child throws a tantrum about a candy bar at the checkout line, and you give them a candy bar just to make them be quiet and stop the stares that are inevitably coming your way from other parents, then you are actively rewarding negative behavior. The child will see this, realize that a certain behavior got a certain reward, and it will create a loop in their brain that will trigger them to react in a similar way the next time.

Imagine the same scenario at home, when there are fewer stares and more time to flesh out the situation. If you tell your child to go clean their room, then that same loop will play again inside the brain and make them throw a tantrum in hopes of you relenting. Only here, the stakes are different. There are no stares, no impatient customers behind you waiting to check out, and the perceived "cost"—a candy bar is not really that expensive, is it?—is nonexistent. In that scenario, it does not matter to you whether you stand there for two minutes or two days; you are going to win, after all.

This disconnect is what rebellious children feed on. The lack of consistency from a parent's discipline creates confusion inside a child that does not allow them to process situations appropriately. While absolutely nobody likes to fight the grocery store scenario, giving in on even a minor thing like that can cause huge repercussions down the road. In their eyes, it is not them that is the problem, it is you. You are the one that is inconsistent, you are the one that is unjust, and you are the one that needs to bend, not them.

A rebellious child may also amp up their own aggressiveness in response to a parent's increased aggression. In the same scenario outlined above, if a child asks for a candy bar and you say no, and then they start throwing a fit, only to have you raise your voice and get more aggressive, you can also create a situation where you both end up in a shouting match over something as minuscule as a $0.99 bar of chocolate. What that child has learned is that conflict in the house is solved by fighting amongst each other, not by rational, authoritative conversation. You are feeding the monster, so do not be surprised when, over time, that monster grows.

Think of strong-willed children as participating in a team sport alongside their parents. They are tough and usually demanding; that is mostly because they expect everyone in the family to rise to their level. Even though they perceive themselves as the ones in charge, there is no doubt that their demanding attitude is due to trying to get everybody else to rise to their level. Strong-willed children will, over time, become a strong asset, whereas a rebellious child will create a division inside the home because they feel like there is no place for them. To be a part of the team, you have to work with them, not against them. In this scenario, a rebellious child is not the product of themselves, but of the parent. Think on that.

If you observe other parents who have notoriously strong-willed children, what you may notice is that 90% of the parent's attention goes to correcting wrong behaviors, while 10% (or even less) goes toward rewarding good behaviors. If all a child hears time and time again is how they need to not do something, there is no incentive for them to do the right thing. Part of the growth process of a parent that wants to mold a strong-willed child and keep the rebellious kid at bay, is more often than not by reinforcing good behaviors. They need to feel like you are on the same team as them, or they will continue to drive a wedge inside the family.

I have said it before, and I'll say it again: having a strong-willed child can be a blessing. What you are raising is not a bad kid that will fight everyone at the drop of a hat, but a person with a strong moral compass that believes ardently in a set of rules. With the right training, that child can be a strong ally for you later in life and to the people they surround themselves with. They are seen as assets, not liabilities, despite how they are perceived at the moment.

Chapter 3: Why Your Child's Strong Will is a Blessing

There was a world-famous experiment done in the early '70s by a professor at Stanford University that wanted to test whether or not certain developmental traits seen early in life led to success down the road. In this situation, researchers put a bunch of children one at a time into a room. In front of the child, they placed a single marshmallow and were given two options: either eat it now, or wait and get a second one when the researcher returned fifteen minutes later.

As you can imagine, many kids gobbled up the first marshmallow without thinking twice. Others, conscience of the reward that was to be theirs later if they simply waited, refused to eat the marshmallow. They were certainly impatient though, playing with their fingers, singing songs, and in some cases, even turning their chair completely around so that they did not face the temptation. When the researcher came back in, they rewarded those children with the second marshmallow.

Over the years, the Stanford researchers tracked the progress of those children, and found that the ones who had waited usually achieved greater success in life, such as taking leadership positions in business or becoming collegiate-level athletes. The common denominator among them was the ability to delay gratification. Consciously choosing to wait now in order to receive a bigger prize later is not easy, but it can develop hard work, discipline, and patience inside the individual.

I tell you this story not so that you can set your kid in a room and put a marshmallow in front of him to see whether or not he'll turn out to be the CEO of a Fortune 500 company someday, but as a lesson to you, the parent. I know good and well that one of the biggest temptations for any parent is to make their child a top performer every single day, and while that may be a somewhat admirable goal, the reality is that your child simply cannot live by that standard all the time. There will be tough times, and there will be even tougher times, but if you are patient, they will all lead you to a future that you and your child can both be proud of.

There are no words to express how terrible I feel watching parents struggle with their children in everyday life. As a therapist, I usually see people in two different arenas: in my office, and in the real world.

In my office, we can work through things together and I can give the parents strategies and tactics that they can use to later help their child. In the real world, I'm forced to watch as parents unsuccessfully try to negotiate with their children, discipline them severely, or—in the absolute worst case—ignore their kids completely. I cannot help the situation, and it tears me apart.

But that is nothing compared to what I know that child is going through. As we'll discuss in a later chapter, what your strong-willed child needs more than anything else in the entire world is your trust. They need to feel free to make their own decisions—under your watchful eye, of course—and feel like they have some autonomy over their life. Too many parents, told that they need to exert their own authority over their children in some misguided way to earn their respect, try to coerce their children into submission. It almost never works.

Don't get me wrong, I am a big fan of disciplining your child to learn to respect authority. But just as importantly, your child needs to learn to trust themselves. In the end, it is only going to be them that has to deal with the world each day when you are not around, so how will they do it? Will they constantly call you and ask your opinion about what they are going to have for lunch, or will they learn to stand on their own two feet and make their own decisions?

That is why, as often as I can, I remind parents that their strong-willed child is a blessing. It is a gift, in the purest sense of the word, and one that is entrusted only to parents that are actually able to handle it.

In my opinion, the absolute best part about having a strong-willed child is that you know exactly where they stand on absolutely everything (conversely, this is also what makes them so difficult to live with most of the time). Since strong-willed children are so prone to expressing their opinions and demanding that certain things be changed to their liking, there is absolutely zero guessing as to what they are thinking on any particular subject. You know how they feel about people, about possessions, about certain life events, and their own emotions. Kids go through so many different ups and downs in their young life that the ability to witness those changes happening in real time is one of the greatest blessings you will ever have - chiefly because you will be able to help them navigate it.

This cooperation will bring you and your family together and stronger than ever before. Easy-going children are great, but few things make a husband and wife pull together like those long, deep conversations about how to handle their strong-willed child. I'm not sure what the stats are on marriage survival rates among people with especially difficult children (or even if such data exists in the first place), but I would imagine it's pretty good. Usually, when I'm talking to parents about their strong-willed child, I'm not talking to just one, I'm talking to both of them. They work together because they have a common goal of helping their child to succeed. It is a beautiful thing.

I have also seen the same parents express an amazing amount of compassion to other parents. They say that you can never truly help somebody who is going through a part of their life unless you have gone through it yourself, and that maxim is especially true about parents of difficult children. They almost never compare theirs to others—except in moments of weakness—and are usually the first ones to extend a loving shoulder when another parent just needs to vent. This compassion is seen by their children, who will go on to become some of the most compassionate people as well, keeping the cycle moving ever forward.

But enough about parents - what about the children that are strong-willed themselves? What makes them so great?

As we have alluded to a few times so far, these children usually grow up to be extremely independent, persistent, and fearless. For a four-year-old, those are not always the most desirable traits, as that independence can cause them to wander off in the middle of a hardware store while you frantically search for them. In other situations, that fearlessness may make them jump off a trampoline onto the ground below, just to see if they can do it. As you are sitting there in the emergency room with them afterwards, you might curse the heavens for bringing you this child in the first place.

But just think about what that child will grow up to be. If you follow the biographies of some of the most esteemed inventors, businesspeople, and explorers, there is example

25

after example of these types of people sprouting from otherwise rebellious existences. Mark Zuckerberg was nearly kicked out of Harvard for starting Facebook. Steve Jobs refused to shower and wear shoes during his entry-level position at Atari. Matt Damon and Ben Affleck dropped out of college to move to Hollywood and try and sell the screen rights for a little movie called Good Will Hunting. I don't know their parents, but I would imagine every last one of them shook their heads in dismay as they watched their kids take these enormous—and possibly ill-calculated—risks.

Today, they are all smiles. I'm not suggesting that your child will grow up to be the next tech billionaire, but what I am suggesting is that your child's independent and stubborn streak may very well be what makes the difference in the open market. While others are struggling to find jobs during a tough recession—of which this generation knows too much about—strong-willed children will not only buck the system to keep pushing for what they want, but will also think outside the box for creative solutions. Those very attributes that you reviled in the emergency room when they were five may eventually come back to save their bacon twenty years later.

Without going too far off the cliché path, you mustn't think that your child's strong-willed nature is an end unto itself. It may very well be a necessary steppingstone to create the life that not only they were born to have, but were put on this earth to impact the world with as well.

And that is a blessing that is all their own.

Chapter 4: How Your Kid Learns Most Effectively

Okay, enough of these gooey-Kumbaya feelings. How do you get these kids to the point in their lives where they are not only successful, but truly happy? After all, is not that part of what our job is as parents?

It might not need to be said at this stage in the game, but strong-willed children learn very differently than the other kids they share recess with. While those kids may sit and listen to instructions, following them with glee, your kid may stare-off into the distance, plotting their own direction in life without giving a second thought to what is being asked of them. In fact, the only reason they may actually listen to the authority figure in the room is so that they can do the exact opposite.

Before we go into the psychological effects of what makes a strong-willed child today, we have to say a few words about how environment plays into that situation. In today's world, screen-time is more of an issue than ever before. Kids are constantly on tablets, consuming media through phones, TV, or the Internet, and those environmental factors are molding their outlook on life. While it is nearly impossible to restrict access to these devices all the time, what you can do is limit the amount of time and what they are viewing.

Kids that are under the age of seven have a really difficult time separating what they are viewing on screen from the reality that they see in everyday life. If they watch an especially violent movie, for instance, they may think that is the way the world works, and at an age where their minds are so easily malleable, these impressions can stay with them for a lifetime. We talked about choosing your battles earlier; this is a battle that you must win.

As some scientists are starting to point out, it may be that the most damaging aspect to your child's developmental process is not what they are viewing on screen, but what they are not doing in everyday life. If your kid is spending hours every single day on a device, it takes away from time that they could be using to develop creativity, imagination, and role-playing abilities. This type of imaginative play is vital to every kid's learning, and it is your job as a parent to help foster that as much as possible.

Other environmental factors will come into play as well, such as the amount of sleep they are getting or the stresses that exist inside the family. Statistically speaking, divorce is one of the most dramatic things that a child can go through, and as they are watching the fabric of their very existence be torn in half, they will inevitably react in very negative ways. Do not be surprised if this causes several disruptions in their personality, although hopefully it will not be permanent.

As with everything though, the real determining factor in environmental stressors is how it is handled inside the family. If your children watch you go through a tough time with anger, resentment, backbiting, and hatred, they will model these same behaviors in their lives. They will start to believe that all conflict in their own life is resolved by less than desirable means, which can make the strong-willed tendencies even more deliberate. If there are situations in your family that are spiraling out of control, make a special effort to treat them with civility, and spend time talking to your child to make sure they feel loved.

If there is one way that all kids learn—strong-willed kids especially—it is through modeling others' behavior. Just like the candy store incident that we talked about earlier, kids learn through replicating patterns that they see in the world around them. If someone they see gets a reward because of a certain action that they perform, you can bet that they will mimic that exact behavior to get what they want as well.

What this means for you as a parent is twofold: first, you must be aware of who your kid's friends are, and you also must be aware of how you appear to your child. If you are aggressive, domineering, dismissive, and judgmental, you can bet that your child will be the same way. Furthermore, if the friends that your kids associate with are known to be rule breakers, they could start to copy their behavior. Instead of forcing your child to stay away from certain people, as a parent you must create an environment that fosters the positivity and behaviors you want them to have. By their very nature, you cannot simply tell kids what to do; you must let them make the decisions for themselves.

That does not mean that you can't control the environment they exist in, though. Create opportunities for your child to interact with positive role models and watch programs that reinforce good behavior, and you will be a lot better off in the long run.

Chapter 5: Why You Should Resist the Temptation to "Break" Them

I have a friend that shoes horses in the panhandle of Texas. The ranch that he works on is vast, and consists of hundreds of acres of grassland, which is home to many different animals. Whenever they get a horse that is either young or especially stubborn, their first order of business is to "break" them.

I'm never around during this process, but the way my friend has described it to me is exceedingly slow and painful. First, they will start by showing the horse that needs be broken how a horse is to be ridden in the first place. They will pick one that is already well behaved, climb on top of it, and ride it around the yard in front of the other horse. After that, they will slowly introduce the concept of a saddle by letting the horse wear it for a few minutes at first, then adding more time to it as the horse get more comfortable. Once comfortable with the saddle, they will usually try to ride the horse alongside a few other well-trained horses so that the unbroken one can get a feel for what it means to be ridden.

At least, that is the way it is supposed to go. From what I have heard, horses do not always take to the saddle as easily as this 1-2-3 step process. In fact, they will mostly buck the saddle several times while my friend tries to put it on, sometimes taking days, weeks, or even more than a month to allow someone to sit on them comfortably. In the end though, it is always worth it. What you have after this process is a fiery horse that has been tamed, allowing it to be not mastered by its emotions, but instead receive instructions from an authority figure.

Now, what would happen if you took the same saddle, threw it on the same horse, and then tried to hop on its back? How long do you think it would take before you were thrown off, landing face first in a pile of mud or other "stuff"? I would give it anywhere between 5 to 10 seconds at most before you found a very painful and humiliating end.

All horses need to be broken, but there is an easy way and a hard way to do it. One is through a gentle, consistent process of introducing new conditions, while the other is just throwing everything together and hoping that something sticks. One way will most certainly end up with a happy and content horse, even though it may take longer, while the other will result in two entities slowly dancing around each other for months, hoping the other one will break first.

The same is true of you and your child. Most parents look at their strong-willed child as a horse that needs be broken. If they refuse to clean their room, by George, you are gonna make them. If they refuse to do their homework, you will buckle them to the chair with a pencil in hand until they finish their math assignment. That is the hard way, and it usually ends up just as humiliating and painful as trying to break a horse in the same manner.

The effect on a child can be enormous. While you may win the battle, you will inevitably lose the war, as not only will your child become more bitter toward you but they will also look for more ways to assert their authority and contrast your own. While they may do their homework, they will also rush through it, writing wrong answers on purpose to show you and the teacher that they do not need any training. Alternatively, they may also sit there for hours at a time, refusing to make even a single mark on the paper in the hopes that you will give up and allow them to eventually go to bed.

You do not need me to tell you that this situation is bad. Strong-willed children love struggle, and this is just another opportunity for them to flex their own muscles in comparison to yours. They will win, one way or the other.

In reality, though, everyone loses. The child loses because they are not taught the importance of getting their homework done, and the parent loses because they end up (a) sleep-deprived and (b) frustrated and unsure of what to do next. The next day will bring about another battle, and all the parents can hope for is that they win that one too.

But is "winning" what is really most important here? If you think of your child as a horse that needs to be "broken" so that it can allow you to be the authority figure, then you will not only *not* end up with a submissive child, but you will also end up with an ill-tempered, shy, and possibly even skittish child as well. Your child will be "broken" all right—just not in the sense that you wanted him or her to be.

Rome wasn't built in a day, but too often I have heard a parent in my office say they are going to "lay down the law" for a period of time in order for their child to understand who's in charge. While this may seem like a noble idea— dedicating yourself to more intensive parenting for a period of time—the effect on the child is nothing short of culture shock. One day, the parent is a passive, sometimes present figure in their life, and the next day, the parent is all "up in their business," to quote a term from the '90s. They go from aloof to smothering, and the child never knows how to react. Is this the new norm? Will their every move be monitored? If so, how are they supposed to retain their sense of individuality?

At the heart of every strong-willed child is an independent streak, just like mustangs that have lived most of their lives in the wild. They developed their own sense of self and have crafted their habits by their surroundings in order to survive. Going from one extreme to the other will only cause your child to react negatively, which embitters the parent further, causing them to either double down on the discipline, or ignore them completely.

The truth is, horses aren't broken, and neither are children. Each of them is taught through example to be a part of a team, and it requires an enormous amount of patience and dedication to integrate that free spirit into the part of a larger cohort. Parents that I have seen be most successful with raising strong-willed children are the ones that dedicate themselves to being just 1% better each day. Making a small commitment to acknowledge your child's positive traits, spending time with them, or empowering them to grow always results in the best results over time.

Here's a fact that you can take to the bank: whoever your child will become is ultimately a reflection of the relationship that we build with them. If that relationship is built on anger, stern discipline, harsh words, or an attempt to break their spirit, they might relent for a period of time, but I guarantee you it will come out in horrid ways down the line. More than once I have seen a child go from quiet and submissive to a total rebel and rule breaker, leaving the parents to wonder where they went wrong. Most the time, I can help them navigate to a point in their life where they made the decision to tear down their child's spirit, instead of helping to craft it in the manner that it should go.

To be sure, it is a temptation to assert your dominance over your child, but it is one that you should fight whenever possible. Make no mistake, you are the authority figure in the house, but only a true leader understands that an organization works best when those at the top of the food chain are servants to those at the bottom. If "winning" is your goal, then by all means, try to break them. But if you want to develop a well-rounded individual who can be a valuable member to society, consider how you can be an example to them each day.

Chapter 6: The One Thing Your Child Craves More Than Anything

Have you ever seen a kid in a toy store? Granted, most independent toy chains are now dinosaurs from the past, but if you have ever seen a modern child swoop through the toy section of an online retailer, you know the gleam in their eye that comes from seeing a toy that they can buy. They will beg the parent, plead with the parent, and in some cases, even put together a PowerPoint presentation to show why they deserve the treat (it is true, I have seen it myself).

I do not question their desire, but as every parent knows, the toys they so earnestly plead for one day end up at the bottom of the toy chest the next. They have either replaced it with a shiny new object to play with, or they have exhausted all of its functionality and see no purpose for it in their life. Either way, that money, while not really wasted, is gone.

What does your child really want, though? I have asked that question to hundreds of parents before, only to be met with blank stares and hem-haws around an answer. I have seen the deer in the headlights look that they give me when I tell them that what their child really craves is not toys, candy, or really even independence. What every strong-willed child craves more than anything else in the world—is your trust.

That may seem silly; after all, who would trust a six-year-old to make decisions for their life? They are still at least ten years away from driving and being able to vote, so why would we allow them, in good conscience, to make decisions that will determine their future?

To ask that question is to answer it. Kids need to feel free to make mistakes, and more importantly, to learn from those mistakes. A strong-willed child, by definition, does not learn best when they are told what to do on a blackboard; they learn the most when they experience certain things. By the same token, I would argue that most kids learn that way, and most adults do as well. For instance, learning French through an app on your phone is fine, but if you really want to learn proper French, you need to plop yourself down in a café in Paris and listen to the conversations around you. That is the same experiential learning that your child needs, albeit on a smaller scale.

Before we go any further, listen to what I'm telling you. I am not saying that you need to give in to every single whim that your child has. The last thing you need to do is give your kids the keys to their life and sit back and watch them crash. You will always be a stabilizing and guiding influence in their life, but only if they feel like they are free to make their own decisions. Things like bedtime, meals, and even cleaning always have more leeway than we care to admit. While we would prefer them to eat every last vegetable that is on the plate, I know most parents would be happy if they finished just half of them. And if not, we can stack the deck in our favor by putting more vegetables on their plate in the hope that they will finish half, which actually ends up being about the regular portion anyway. See how that works?

How does this play out in the real world? Consider our example of the child in the grocery line that wants a candy bar. You may, using your own judgment, allow them to have that candy, but only if they clean their room first whenever they get home. In their mind, they will view the situation honestly: Is it worth it to me to clean my room for the candy bar, or would I rather avoid the work and the reward together? It is a negotiation tactic, obviously, but one in which all parties win.

The benefit of this is that your children will inevitably learn from their mistakes. A child who insists on wearing hot fleece pajamas to bed at night in the middle of summer will learn very quickly that the decision they made was a foolish one. The parent may spend hour after hour trying to convince them to dress more appropriately, but by allowing them to make a tiny mistake without immediate correction, you will teach them to consider their options more carefully in the future. While they may get their way now, there's a good chance they'll realize later that getting their way is not always necessarily the best option.

But what have they ultimately learned? For one, they will realize that you are not as dumb as they may think. You have experience that you can share with them, and I guarantee you the next interaction will have them be a little bit more lenient on their part. Instead of outright refusing to wear what you laid out for them, they may at least ask why.

I'll be honest here, this is not going to be easy for you. Most parents have been conditioned to see themselves as the final decision-maker on every single thing that happens underneath their roof (to be fair, other parents just do not care, but that's a conversation for another time). They cannot fathom the idea of letting their child make their own decisions but doing so not only establishes a system of trust between you and the child, but also allows them to grow in experiential learning that is so vital at a young age. Learning to make your own decisions, and handling the consequences of those decisions, is an important trait that everybody needs to learn, so they might as well learn it while they are young.

What this will require from you more than anything else is the ability to get perspective on the situation with your children. Take a step back and look at the world through their eyes. They do not see things that happened on the news, or the stock prices going up and down, or the possibly contentious election cycles that we have day in and day out.

The only thing that they are concerned about in their little world is whether or not they get to stay up an extra 30 minutes to play with the blocks. When you see the world through their eyes, you understand that the emotions they feel are just as real as the ones that you and I feel, even if in our eyes, they seem puny by comparison. But as we talked about earlier, comparing your child to anybody else, including yourself, is a recipe for disaster. Only by looking at the world through their eyes can we hope to help them make the decisions that are best for them.

Think of yourself as a guiding force in this process. Instead of asserting your authority over them and saying "my way or the highway," help them through the decision-making process. If they reject the pajamas that you lay out for them in the middle of summer, ask them how comfortable they think they will be in the fleece ones. Ask them if they think they will be hot later in the night, since it is so hot outside. Finally, when all else fails, make a compromise with them that you leave out the ones that they should be wearing on their bed just in case they change their mind. Kids love having this level of independence, but most importantly, they love the trust they receive from their parents. It makes them feel included and special, which is the best kind of positive reinforcement you can get.

Of course, in order for them to feel like they can trust you, you also have to be a person of your word. If you set a reward for them if they follow through on something, make sure you deliver. Likewise, if you set consequences for them if they refuse, make sure you follow through on that. While it may be tough and seem counterproductive to everything we have talked about so far, knowing there are clear boundaries that they have in their life is fundamental—as long as they know you are willing to talk to them.

It is no surprise that respect and honesty are two of the hallmarks of our civilization (or, at least, they should be). We value kids for who they are and treat their opinions about the world as valid, no matter how silly they may seem to us. I can remember vividly asking my child why he didn't finish his potatoes one night, when he decided to branch off into his personal philosophy about whether or not Power Rangers were stronger than Transformers. Despite the fact that his line of reasoning was invalid (Transformers will always beat the Power Rangers, hands down), it had absolutely nothing to do with what we were talking about at the time. Nevertheless, by allowing him to talk about what was important to him in that moment, he respected me when I gently reminded him to finish his potatoes. He did not eat all of them, but he ate most of them, and then we played with his toys on the floor afterward. I call that a win, and so would any honest parent as well.

Chapter 7: Is It ADHD?

I hate labels.

In fact, the thought of even addressing a book specifically to "strong-willed children" initially unnerved me, primarily because I do not believe that any one child is this or that. As we discussed several times so far, each child—to a certain extent—is a product of their environment. Strong-willed children aren't necessarily better or worse than every other child, since every child creates their own unique challenges.

That being said, there is such a thing as Attention-Deficit/Hyperactivity Disorder (ADHD), and since the parents of so many strong-willed children have asked me if their child should be diagnosed with it, I felt it best to include a chapter talking about whether or not you should seek further testing for your child.

I found that many parents are quick to put a label on their child in order to give them some kind of a baseline to work with. In the face of a mounting list of challenges, parents want to have a starting block to shoot from; some kind of foundation by which they can build from to treat their children. These intentions are mostly well-placed, but if your kid does not actually have ADHD, these intentions can be ineffective at best, and damaging at worst.

The first thing that we need to say about ADHD is that it is really nothing new. There are predecessors that date back 100+ years in our nation's history, even including some very notable figures that we would regard as geniuses today, such as Thomas Edison and Albert Einstein. Even modern-day figures such as Simone Biles, Justin Timberlake, and Ty Pennington have been diagnosed with ADHD, so having the diagnosis is no more prohibitive to a fulfilling and successful life than anything else. It is just a matter of how you handle it.

It wasn't until the 1970s and 1980s at the actual term of Attention-Deficit/Hyperactivity Disorder really came to the public's attention. Recognized by the American Psychiatric Association in the late 1960s, there are articles that date back as far as the 18th century that describe situations and conditions are eerily similar to ADHD. In fact, there were a whole host of other names given to what we now call ADHD, such as "defective moral control," "brain dysfunction," and even "incapacity of attending with the necessary degree of constancy to anyone object." Try putting that on a medical form today.

Today, ADHD is a universally accepted condition that affects nearly 5% of school-age children, and most often boys, who are three times more likely to be diagnosed than girls. Chances are, you either know someone with ADHD, or your child does. It is thought that there is at least one child with ADHD in every single classroom in America.

What makes diagnosing a child with ADHD especially difficult is that it mimics so many other behavioral traits that are seen in children everywhere. The fact that a child cannot concentrate on a lesson on the whiteboard, for instance, may not actually mean that they have ADHD—it may just mean that they have a problem sitting still. In that case, it needs to be treated as a behavioral problem, not necessarily a "condition."

This is especially true with parents who have strong-willed children. Things such as learning disorders, depression, and anxiety are hallmarks of both strong-willed children and kids with ADHD, which is why so many people end up in my office confused about the two. The difference between these two, at least in terms of impact, is just as muddled. Both types of children respond in similar ways in classrooms and inside the family unit. They may be aloof, demanding, unable to sit still, and have a remarkably short attention span. Regardless of the "label," these types of behaviors need to be handled some way.

It is also hard to diagnose because no single trait defines kids with either ADHD or having a strong will. Instead, it is more of a hodgepodge of different behavioral traits that a trained clinician must look at and identify as one or the other. Normally, most of these traits that we have talked about so far will go away on their own by the kid's third or fourth birthday, but if a child is five or six years old and is still dealing with a severely decreased attention span and a hyperactive personality, it might be time for further study.

Parents are usually quick to claim an ADHD diagnosis mostly because they have no frame of reference for anything else. Parents will describe their children as "very active" or "does not listen" or something similar, without giving any thought to whether or not kids their age—and, more specifically, kids their own age in their specific environment—act the same way. I always encourage parents to examine the types of people that surround your kids the most; if your kid acts like they do, it may not be a psychiatric issue as much as an environmental problem.

Obviously, parents also see their own kids way more than they see other children. They are (or should be) very dialed in on their kids' behaviors, and if even the slightest hair is out of place, it is perceived as a flaw. Parents of strong-willed children, who have battled these issues for years, will insist that their kids need some kind of help, when neither I nor anybody else notice any issues whatsoever. While keeping a close eye over your child's behavior is important, be sure that it does not get to the point of neuroticism—for your own sake, and that of your child.

Generally speaking, there are three primary personality traits for you to watch for. Inattentiveness is one of the biggest, and is mostly identified when the child struggles in school. They usually cannot focus long enough to complete tasks that are assigned to them by authority figures, which negatively impacts the grades. This is why children with ADHD usually perform lower in school; it is not because they are not as smart, but simply because they do not have the patience to actively sit and listen. This does not apply when they are watching a screen, however. Kids with ADHD can watch programming for hours and never take their eyes off the screen, but the second that they are required to do any form of active listening is when the problems start.

You may also notice a strong impulsive desire in your child. Both strong-willed children and those with ADHD react before somebody stops talking, have a hard time waiting in line for games at school, and completely ignore boundaries that are set by others. For this reason, children with ADHD are usually seen as being intrusive; unfortunately, when they are told this, they react negatively. Any perceived slight in their direction is met with hostility, whether aggressive or passive, as the child does not usually know how to handle the situation. In some situations, this impulsivity may bring them into danger themselves. A stray ball that rolls into the street, for instance, is chased without giving a second thought to the danger that the situation presents.

As you can probably tell from the title itself, children with ADHD are very hyperactive as well. The words that are most commonly associated with them are "fidgety," "active," or "always on the go." They cannot sit still, talk nonstop, and the idea of spending ten seconds sitting in a chair is an absolute eternity to them. Trying to get them to sit in the chair once they have gotten up is even tougher, inevitably resulting in disciplinary measures by the school.

We have already mentioned it once, but I feel compelled to say it again: children with ADHD are not problem children. Just like anybody else that has a certain disorder, it needs to be managed, and in most cases, can be managed very effectively. The big question is whether or not the parent is willing to put in the time and the effort to take care of it.

Probably the most frustrating aspect of children with ADHD is where these traits come from in the first place. People have pointed to all sorts of different factors, such as too much screen time, poor diet, or other environmental factors, but most of the science concludes that these children are simply genetically predisposed toward these behaviors. In that sense, there is not much you can do about prevention. You must handle it once the situations start presenting themselves.

The process of diagnosing ADHD is pretty straightforward, albeit somewhat subjective. It involves checklists, interviews, observations, and a whole set of questionnaires that are filled out not just by the parent, but by anybody that has any form of authority in the child's life, such as a teacher or religious counselor. In many cases, the clinician will insist on observing the child for a period of time themselves in order to make a more certain diagnosis.

So, what is a parent to do if their strong-willed child is not diagnosed with ADHD? Honestly, the treatment is very similar for both. Children with ADHD may require medication to function normally, but those effects are usually short-term at best. What parents of all children need to have in their arsenal is a long-term solution to behavioral issues. One-on-one interaction between the parent and the child is the single best thing that anybody can do to help, regardless of whether or not your child has ADHD or just a strong-willed nature.

You must resist the temptation to "outsource" this to a therapist, playgroup, or even a teacher. Kids learn best when their immediate environment (a.k.a. the home) is one that fosters positivity and structure. Furthermore, this instruction works best when it is performed by the person that they trust the most in their life (a.k.a. the parent or guardian). You are the one that needs to set up the type of environment they can escape in, not because they are trying to hide, but because they are trying to build character.

How do you do that? It's simple. Restructure your entire family life from top to bottom and change everything about the way you live.

Just kidding.

Kind of.

Chapter 8: Restructuring the Family Life

I want you to imagine the average life of an American in the late 1800s. Regardless of whether or not you were part of a city or lived on a farm, there are a few ways in which the America of the past is completely different than that of today. For starters, they did not even have a radio, much less a TV or an iPad. The Internet would have been viewed as a mystical act of sorcery in an age where a message transmitted over a wire—known as a telegram—was seen as groundbreaking. Trains were in operation, but few people rode them every single day, and cars were just barely beginning to enter the minds of a few select inventors.

Electricity wasn't nearly as common as it is today (or as it would be at the turn-of-the-century) which meant many families relied on candles and fireplaces to generate any form of light. When the sun was down, you slept, or else you just sat in the darkness and stared at each other. Sitting around a common source of light was usually enough for most people to feel like they were a part of a group, as they shared the events of the day with each other. Families bonded and communities grew together based on geographic proximity. With little else to get in the way of everyday life, people talked to other human beings face-to-face, instead of sitting back on their phones and scrolling through social media, interacting with people through digital means.

The family unit was different, there is no escaping it. Regardless of whether or not you view that as a good thing or a bad thing, the fact remains that people in the 19th century just did not live the way that we do today. There are infinitely more things vying for our attention, with little chance to slow down and simply get to talk to each other. Moreover, there was an abundance of family-oriented traditions that bound them even closer, such as telling stories and sharing family meals. Altogether, these aspects contributed to a strong sense of family that fostered the growth of the individual inside a larger unit.

Without making that time period sound too romantic—the average life expectancy was around 40 years old, after all—it was a simpler time for most people. With fewer screens to stare at and some kind of housework that needed to get done on an almost round-the-clock basis, kids learned how to occupy themselves with the world around them, as well as feeling a sense of responsibility and autonomy—two things that strong-willed children desperately need in today's world.

Kids need to feel that they belong inside of a family unit—that they have a place they can make their own and contribute. For strong-willed children, this need is dialed up even further; while some kids will adjust quickly to not having those things, strong-willed children demand it, sometimes forcefully. While you do not need to be at your children's beck and call at all hours of the day, one of the best things you can do to create a well-rounded individual is to restructure your family environment in a way that includes every single member of the family.

Very few parents that I talk to realize they are doing this consciously, and so, because of that, you may have scoffed at that last comment: "Of course all of my family is included in my day-to-day life. Why wouldn't they be?" And yet, when

I talk to the kids individually, without the watchful eye of their parents, what they usually express to me is the belief that they do not know where they fit in. They go to school, but they feel somewhat like an outcast. They come home and are bossed around by an authority figure. They look at their siblings and recognize that they are playing nicely, but they may not enjoy the same type of activities their siblings engage in. It is a struggle for identity, more than anything else. In that sense, how different are they from the rest of us?

In today's world, there's so much to jam into every single day: sports, hobbies, school, extracurricular activities, not to mention screen time, car travels, and, oh yeah, sleep. Trying to put 100 different activities into a single 24-hour day is next to impossible, and most people—no matter the age—struggle to make it all work.

This type of disorganization is unacceptable to a strong-willed child. For someone who craves routine and autonomy, the feeling of having no ownership over the time in your life is horrifying. As the parent, it is your job to create an environment where they feel they can contribute. Giving them a slice of the family pie may be a struggle at first, especially when you are not sure what it is that they want, but it is one of the best long-term solutions to integrating every person into your family unit. Over time, it'll become second nature.

So, what does this look like on an everyday basis? While the phrase "restructuring the family life" may sound intimidating, it can be summed up in a single word: routine. As we'll talk about later in this book, strong-willed children crave structure more than just about anything else. They want to feel like there is some sense of order in their life, and they want to know what is going to happen throughout the day, and honestly, throughout the rest of the week or even the month. Having a pattern and routines and cycles and organization helps them adapt in a world that is increasingly chaotic and unpredictable. Instead of going with the flow, they demand that the universe bends to them.

This rigidity may make them hard to deal with, especially in comparison to other children who are more laid-back, but once you recognize what areas your child pays specific attention to, it can be remarkably easy. A standard bedtime every night is one routine that many families struggle with, and it can make a world of difference in the life of your child. Eating meals together, normally around the same time, also helps tremendously. Once the child feels like there is some sort of control in their life, you will notice a huge change in their behavior.

Inevitably, what this results in is more time spent together as a family, which is the end goal anyway. As we discussed with children who have ADHD, medications can only do so much; ultimately, the responsibility is on you as a parent to create an environment that helps them grow.

Below are some things that you can incorporate into your schedule. While you may be doing some of these already, making this an intentional part of your life is the key.

- *Have Fun Together.* Many families enjoy game nights, walks in their neighborhood, or just time spent in the backyard throwing a frisbee around. Others, wanting a little bit more adventure in their lives, will go on short vacations or explore different parts of their town. It doesn't really matter what you do, as long as you are together and the kid enjoys it. This is also an excellent opportunity to give them some authority to make choices.

Give them a few options of what you can do as a family and let them choose. Also, it doesn't have to always be about them; create a rotation where every child picks the activity for the day or the week.

• *Have Fun Separately.* Children need unstructured playtime built into their daily lives. Decades ago, before the advent of smart phones and video game systems, children enjoyed a lot more free play than they do these days. When children rely on screens to do the entertaining for them, they do not use their brains to actively create worlds and scenarios to learn from. What children really need to do is to develop their imagination, observing the world and interacting with it in a way that they can create different environments. But just because this is called "unstructured play time" does not mean that you can take your hands off the wheel. You will have to remove electronic devices and screens and allow them to truly be children, which means going outside and creating their own adventures. Strong-willed children have a tendency to rail against authority, so having free time that they can decide what to do with on their own is extremely important to feeling a sense of self-worth.

• *Explain Constantly.* It can be extremely difficult to handle a strong-willed child that is constantly rebelling at every turn. The temptation is to lay the hammer down on every single occasion where they talk back or refuse to follow your directions. While I would never encourage any child to be disrespectful, what you can do in the moment is explain why you are setting the boundaries where they are. Kids need to know why the rule exists in the first place so that they can follow it easier, and informing them of your actions and why you do them is a tiny thing you can do to that end. If you are replacing the air filter in your home, for instance, use it as an opportunity to explain that there is dirt from the outside that does not need to be inside, and that the air filter helps trap it. Watch as their little eyes stare at you in amazement, pondering where the dirt comes from. It really is amazing to watch your child learn more about the world around them.

- *Praise Consistently.* Strong-willed children are used to hearing what they do wrong. They know that whenever their parents open their mouths, it is usually to tell them to stop doing something instead of to encouraging them forward. By praising your children constantly, even for little things that they do, you will create a positive environment where they do not feel like their every move is being watched and subsequently judged. Watch as they brush their teeth and climb into bed, and give them a high five for doing both of these things properly. If they eat a vegetable that you know they do not like, point it out and tell them how proud you are of them. If they hand you a drawing that they created of something, and it does not reflect the subject even remotely, tell them how beautiful it is anyway and hang it on the refrigerator. You are not raising a Van Gogh, but by encouraging them in their everyday life, they will feel like a superstar regardless.

- *Create routines.* We talked about this a little bit earlier, but children need to have routines in their everyday lives to feel like they have some sense of ownership. But while routines around bedtime, mealtime, and homework time are all acceptable, you can also create traditions that they can lean on. A weekly movie and pizza night, for instance, is one of our family's favorite activities. Our kids used to look forward to it every week. When Friday rolled around, it did not matter what else happened, they knew that we were going to order a pizza and watch a movie as a family. You can have a favorite song that you sing in the car together, or a book that you like to read around a certain time of the year, or an activity that you only do outside. This type of structure will give them a foundation to build on, and one they can turn to when times get tough.

Chapter 9: When in Doubt, Give Options

So, you have overhauled your entire family structure to accommodate routines and traditions that can help foster growth inside your family unit. It is now a place of love and encouragement; one where following directions is reinforced, as is cooperation with other people. Your child is turning into a valuable member of society where they do not necessarily rebel at every opportunity, instead choosing to work through their emotions with the help of people that they trust and love.

Do you believe me? I did not think so.

While the above scenario may sound idyllic, the reality for most parents is far from that. Most will struggle day in and day out with a strong-willed child, as the emotions and interruptions of day-to-day life threaten to undo every single thing that they have worked for. While you may be trucking along nicely with your kid, giving encouragement where it is necessary and allowing them to explore their own space, at some point, you will find yourself between the proverbial rock and a hard place.

So, what you do when all your routines and structure and traditions break down, and you are left with the screaming child on the floor that refuses to listen to reason?

Give them options.

Very few things in life can be classified accurately as a silver bullet, but I strongly believe that allowing your child to have options every single day is one of the best ways to not only give them what they want, but what you want as well. It is a win-win for both parties, and I have seen it work wonders in situations where parents are left without any other tool in their arsenal.

By definition, a strong-willed child is strong-willed because they have a strong will (imagine that). What they want to do butts up against what you want them to do, and though giving them what they want is the easiest way to quell the immediate problem, it does not give itself over to long-term growth. By giving your child options between two desirable outcomes, you stack the deck in your own favor. No matter which one they choose, you win, and in their mind, they won too.

Maybe an example will help. Let's say you've told your four-year-old that she needs to clean up the room before going to bed. As children do, little Susie most likely refuses to do so, contentedly playing with her toys on the middle the living room floor while the paint in her bedroom slowly peels off the walls because of how dirty the room is.

"Susie, you need to remember to clean your room before you go to bed, got it?" you say.

No response.

"Susie, did you hear me?" Your voice is getting a little louder now, as you get more and more agitated. You have seen how this story ends, and you are not a fan.

"Yep."

"So, are you gonna do it?" you ask innocently.

"Nah," she responds without looking up. "I'll do it tomorrow."

As you stand there staring at your child, watching all your hard work in training and encouraging little Susie to not be rebellious go up in smoke, remember the last tool in your tool belt: give her an option.

"Okay, that is fine Susie. You can clean it tomorrow if you want, but if you do, you have to go to bed now so you can clean it before I drop you off at daycare."

As the inevitable whining starts to pick up, you butt in and give her a choice. "OR," you say, "I'll let you stay up another ten minutes if you promise to do it tonight. How does that sound?"

She looks up at you to see if you are being serious or just pulling a fast one on her. Once she notices that you are not flinching, she slowly goes back to playing with her toys.

"I'll clean it up tonight if I can stay up for another ten minutes," she says softly.

"Deal," you say as you stretch out your hand for her to shake. You slowly walk back to the living room and plop down in front of the TV, knowing that in ten minutes, not only will she get up and go clean her room, but that she'll also go to bed right after.

But how can you be so sure? After all, there is nothing definite that says you will not have to repeat this process in ten minutes all over again. Technically, that is true, but when you say that, you forget the cardinal rule in dealing with strong-willed children: they have a strong moral center. The world needs to make sense to them, and it needs to have some semblance of control and order, so to break that order, especially when they are the ones that designed it that way in the first place, is almost completely unthinkable. I have seen hundreds of parents utilize a technique like this, and I can count on one hand the number of times it has failed me. Can it happen? Sure. Does it happen? Not nearly as often.

Part of the reason for that is that the child knows that by making such an arrangement, they are the one that are in control. That is not technically true, though. The parent is the one that set the terms and conditions. All the child did was agree to them. By getting to stay up an extra ten minutes, however, the child feels like they have won. By getting the room clean and their child in bed, the parent feels like they have won. Tell me another situation in life that can be as mutually beneficial as that?

Also, did I mention that this little arrangement can be made ten minutes before the child's original bedtime anyways, leading them to not only clean the room but go to bed at the regular time? That is next level parenting right there.

The best part is that you can use this for just about everything, whether you are trying to get your child to do their homework, eat their vegetables, come in from playing outside, putting down the iPad, or whatever else it is it you are trying to get them to do. By giving way a little bit in your rules and allowing them to have a little bit more of what they want, they choose between doing what you want now, or doing what you want a bit later while also getting slightly more of what they want. In their minds, they are in control, which completely breaks down the defenses of the strong-willed child.

But unless you think that this is some kind of parenting ploy that does nothing but manipulate the child and strengthen your own authoritarian position, consider the fact that giving kids a say in everyday situations builds a sense of respect between the two parties. When both sides bend a little to achieve an outcome desirable to everyone, that is called cooperation. It is something that I wish more of our leaders—and more people, in general—employed in their everyday life.

It also strengthens community. Gone are the days in which children are marginalized members of any family units, as those days should be. We should value each member of our family as individuals, giving them a voice and a certain healthy level of respect inside our lives. Allowing them to have a say in the day-to-day operations of our family, however small they might be, strengthens the overall development of our community and our family in general and invites cooperation from all parties. Now, instead of one or two people dictating all the terms of the house, the family works together to decide what is in their best interest under the leadership of the parents or guardians.

Allowing kids to have a say also develops critical problem-solving skills that they will need in everyday life. The ability to analyze a situation and choose the option that benefits you the greatest is a skill. Too many adults are paralyzed by trying to make decisions that should otherwise be very simple. Anyone that has ever been inside of an escape room with a group of other grown adults knows that not everybody has these capabilities, and also knows how valuable they are.

Perhaps most importantly—or more shrewdly, one might say—allowing your kids to have a say between two options capitalizes on your kid's desire to control situations. It is a very simple rule of the jungle: if you find what an animal craves the most, and you control it, you can control the animal.

Now, your strong-willed child is not an animal, obviously, but the point remains the same. Once you discover what your child craves the most—which is most often control—you can engineer scenarios by giving them an ounce of that power. It is not manipulative in any way; it is just a good negotiation tactic that every parent can use to their advantage.

All of that being said, there are a few things we need to keep in mind whenever we give kids options. First and foremost, never overwhelm them with too many decisions. This is a tactic that should only be used a few times every day, otherwise your child becomes wise to the situation and starts to play it to their own advantage. Most importantly, overwhelming them with too many options in a single moment can also backfire, creating the same paralysis that we see sometimes in adults. Never give them more than two—or at the most three—options to choose from at any point in time, or else your child cannot properly compare them to make the best decision.

Second, be consistent in this decision-making process. Do not give them an option today and not give them an option tomorrow. If you make a little bit of an agreement for dinner, be prepared to offer them the same agreement the next day. Doing otherwise will only set you up for disappointment, and increased bitterness when the child realizes that the concession was only for that one time.

Third, think outside the box as to when this tactic can be used at other times. For instance, you do not always need to have a stalemate to produce a scenario for you to give your child options; you can also give them the option of helping around the house, which they are free to decline if they want to. More often than not, your child will jump at the opportunity to help you by carrying a tool or by pointing to a location where a nail needs to be. These small jobs help them feel included and valuable, while also giving them the choice as to whether or not they want to help you. If they do, great; if not, that is fine too. Every little ounce of control and power that you can give them every day will go a long way in helping to head off future struggles.

Finally, be sure to thank them when they decide. Remind them that making a decision is a good thing, but sticking to that decision is even better. Impress upon them the value of cooperation between people in a way that both parties can get what they want, and the next time that you find your back against the wall, you can remind them of these prior situations where you guys cooperated. The absolute last thing you want is a standoff between yourself and your child, so when all else fails, give them options to work through so they can make the best decision for themselves and for you.

Chapter 10: A Day in the Life of YOU

We are rapidly approaching the halfway point of this book, so it makes sense to take a few seconds and think about how the things we talked about so far play into the average day in the life of the parent of a strong-willed child. Understanding these different concepts is one thing, but putting them into actionable, everyday scenarios can be difficult.

Let's start at the beginning, shall we?

6 AM: Wake Up Call

For the purposes of this illustration, we are going to assume that you are a stay-at-home parent whose primary occupation is taking care of children at home—either one or several.

While this can be seen by some as more of a "support" position, I always try to emphasize the fact that being the primary caregiver for children can sometimes be more stressful than your spouse's full-time job, especially if you've got a few strong-willed children at home. In fact, studies have shown that the average mom, for instance, works 98 hours a week—the same as working 2-1/2 full-time jobs. For them, the average mother "clocks in" around 6:30 AM, and "clocks out" at 8:30 PM, seven days a week, 365 days a year.

Just thinking about all the things you have to do in a single day can be an exhausting task, made even more stressful by the fact that you have at least one strong-willed child that is about to rouse from sleep and engage in an all-day battle of wills. Some days are easier than others, but more often than not, you find yourself butting heads with a tiny person that will stop at nothing to get what they want.

Let the day begin.

6:14 AM: Strategy Session

You have a cup of coffee in hand and are slowly scrolling through a list of Facebook status updates, emails, and news apps. While you are caffeinating yourself and finding out what your neighbor thinks about the most recent presidential election, you are also considering the day ahead. What kind of battles will you face today? What appointments are on the docket that you absolutely must be at? Are there any errands that need to be run, such as the grocery store or dry-cleaning pickups?

If so, that needs to be mapped out now. Your strong-willed child needs to have a routine in place so that they know what to expect every single day. It does not need to be ironclad—there is obviously some wiggle room that is inescapable—but they do need to know what to expect. Chances are, they will even ask you about it as soon as they wake up so that they can get a good idea themselves of how to plan their own day.

As you think about your day ahead, consider what worked best for you yesterday. What kind of things did they fight about? Where do you tend to butt heads the most? Also, what minefields could possibly be in your future? A trip to the grocery store needs to avoid the candy section if at all possible, but most stores have the sweets placed up front for that exact reason. They are counting on your child seeing it and wanting it, which results in money out of your pocket. What will you do when that moment comes up? The time to decide that is now.

7:29 AM: Breakfast

Your child is awake and slowly eating the eggs that you have made for him. He tells you about how he slept and what he dreamed about, while you continue to sip your coffee and think about what a sweetheart he is. These are the moments that you treasure; no matter what happens in the future, it is times like this that you can hold near and dear to your heart.

That is, until the first battle takes place.

He's done with his eggs and asks for a banana. You look over at the bananas and notice that they have ripened to the point of being inedible. He doesn't know that though, which means he will continue to fight with you until you give in and give him a banana. After all, you gave him a banana yesterday, so why not today?

Ideally, those bananas would have been thrown in the trash before he saw them, but nobody's perfect. Things happen, so you must deal with that the best way you can.

Start by picking up the bananas and kneeling down next to him. Show him that the bananas are ripe, and even peel a few of them to show him how they are sour and bruised. Once he's had time to analyze it, offer him a replacement— maybe some grapes or strawberries? Apologize for the bananas being bad, and tell him that you will get some more at the grocery store today and that he can have one later if he wants one then.

With any luck, he'll acquiesce, and you will have escaped the first challenge of the day.

8:17 AM: Story Time

Reading should be a part of everybody's day but is especially important for children. Whether that is you reading to him or him learning to sound words out so that he can recognize letters and words, it doesn't really matter. What does matter is that you set some time aside for him to focus just on reading a book and using his imagination.

This is where the line between a strong-willed child and one with ADHD may become more apparent. Children with ADHD may visibly struggle to pay attention and focus, but just be a little fidgety. A strong-willed child, by contrast, may get bored with that book and demand that you go get another one. Resist playing this game. Initially, you can let him go and pick out his own book, or you can give options about which book to pick, but either way, do not fall into the trap of letting him manipulate the situation.

One thing to work on during story time is mastering the ability to read. Strong-willed children love to grow and conquer obstacles, so encourage him not just to listen but to sound out the words and improve his pronunciation. This will ensure that his mind stays engaged with bettering himself, rather than trying to better you.

9:41 AM: Play Time

Unrestricted free time is vital to a child's growth, but it also creates an opportunity for you to rest and recharge for a few minutes. Remove the screens from in front of him and present a variety of different toys or activities for him to do on his own. Even better, let him go in the backyard and create a world that is all his own. Strong-willed children love having their autonomy, so do not hesitate to encourage them to develop it.

Also, take a few seconds to relax. You've earned it.

11:34 AM: Lunch

Whatever your child's nutritional needs are, ask him to help you create a lunch that he would enjoy. Make sure you have healthy options available for him to choose from, but it is not a bad idea to get out of the way and let children create the entire meal themselves (or as much as they can). If they cannot make it themselves, ask them to help you by getting the bread or by putting meat and cheese on the sandwiches, or whatever else they can do.

At some point, he may decide he is done with lunch even though half of it is still sitting on his plate. This is a judgment call for you as to whether or not you will let him get away with it, but if you know he is just being stubborn, allow him to choose between eating it and getting a treat, or throwing the entire thing away now. If he does not finish the food, he does not get a snack—it can be as straightforward as that. Allow him to make his own decision, and then to live with that decision.

1:11 PM: Nap Time

There are some battles that are worth fighting, and for you, nap time may not be one of them. Depending on how old your children are, nap time may be something that they have grown out of completely. Furthermore, the length of naps may be getting shorter and shorter, but no matter how old they are, everybody can benefit from some downtime in the early afternoon, even if it is only for a few minutes.

If napping is essential, but there is always a fight over the location, allow them to determine where and when they nap. Do not force them to go to sleep; all of us have known the frustration of trying to go to sleep and yet being unable to, so you cannot force it on your child any more than you can force it on yourself.

If your child is adamant that he does not want to nap, compromise by letting him play in his room quietly. Who knows, you may walk in there in a little bit and find him fast asleep on the floor. That is okay, because not only did he make the decision to play, but you let him make the decision to fall

64

asleep on his own. Remember, what we are creating is a fully autonomous individual who can make his own decisions. That is the goal. Moments like this help to that end.

3:55 PM: Errands

Probably the hardest part of every day with a strong-willed child is venturing out into the great unknown. You do not know what it is going to be like, you do not know what your child is going to be like, and you have no idea what curveballs the world may throw at you. While you can alleviate some of these by having a plan in place beforehand, your best bet here is to remember to stay calm and not emotionally react to every situation. Instead, think through possible danger spots, and resolve to keep a level head no matter what takes place.

Since the grocery store is usually a hotspot for meltdowns, lay down the ground rules with your child before even walking out the door. Make sure that he is clear on what happens if he does or does not follow them, and make him audibly respond that he understood the terms.

Remind him that you are also going to get bananas—since yours from this morning went bad—and ask him to help you locate them. Ask if he remembers where they are, what shape they are, what color they are, and even let him pick out the bunch inside the store. Any type of ownership you can give to him in this scenario helps.

Once you have finished your shopping and have taken your cart to the front, approach with caution. Chances are your kid is going to see the candy and ask you for it, but respond as patiently and as calmly as possible. If he escalates, then you de-escalate; the last thing you want to do is get into a shouting match with your four-year-old in a public place. Nobody looks good in that situation, least of all you. Remember to be firm, and remind him of the rules that were agreed to before you even walked in. Tears may be streaming down his cheeks, so be sympathetic to the fact that his little heart is broken.

Truthfully, this is where most parents break. In a bid to save face amongst others, they give in to their child's demands in the moment, while making a mental note to work on it in the future. In the absolute worst cases, they give in now only to scold the child later for the behavior. Unless the child is aware of what they are being disciplined for, this type of behavior does nothing more than confuse the child and needs to be avoided at all costs. Kids do not always have the ability to connect why they are being disciplined with certain events, so make sure that they are able to put the dots together. In any case, a calm and reasoned disciplinary action is usually best.

As a side note, this is why God invented grocery pickup. This. Exact. Reason. Do not be afraid to use it.

6:01 PM: Tantrum

As unexpected as a tornado, tantrums can erupt with little to no warning. It can be something you did, something you did not do, or something you did do but did not do in the manner that your child wanted you to. Regardless, they can completely derail a day, and if they happen at the end of the day before the child goes to bed, it leaves a bad taste in your mouth for the next morning.

Like with the grocery store incident earlier, the best thing you can do is to not escalate the situation. Speak to him calmly as if he was an adult and explain the situation to him. Offer him an option to get what he wants and what you want, but if that does not work, you must remain firm. At the end of the day, children need to realize that there is an authority in their lives, and as much as that authority loves them, they also need to learn to respect it. You are the judge here in terms of discipline but remember to keep it fair and balanced. You are the parent, after all.

7:14 PM: Bedtime

The moment has finally arrived—the time when you can reclaim your day for your own and reflect on your time. As you tuck your child in, reflect with him on the high points of the day. Ask him what parts he enjoyed the most and what he would like to do tomorrow. Remind him that you love him and that you cannot wait to spend time with him tomorrow, too.

As you walk out of the room, make a mental note of all the things that he said so that you can incorporate it into the next day's activities. This will help you not only go to sleep tonight knowing that you are prepared for the next day, but will also prove to him that you care about his feelings and that what is important to him is important to you.

Take the rest of the night off. Enjoy the silence.

Chapter 11: How to Not Lose Your Patience

Whew, what a day! Just typing that out was exhausting, so I can only imagine how it feels to be the full-time parent of a strong-willed child day in and day out (actually I do know how it feels, hence this book). It is a struggle every day to feel like you are constantly winning the little battles that will eventually win you the war, so I wanted to take just a quick second and talk about one of the things that I feel is extremely important, yet overlooked by just about every parent out there.

Patience.

No, I'm not talking about developing your child's patience, I'm talking about developing yours. Believe it or not, how you respond to every single situation either amplifies or diminishes your child's negative strong-willed habits. If you intensify the situation in response to his intensification, you can expect the next round to be even worse. Sure, you may quell the immediate issue—and sure enough, many parents tell me with a straight face that yelling over their children works—but you are just setting yourself up for long-term failure.

No matter if your child is strong-willed or not, no parent should ever be in the position of losing their cool in front of their children. Shouting, belittling, or anything else that you can imagine, has no place in a parent-child relationship. Discipline, sure, but do not tear your child down, especially not one who is blessed with a strong will.

Allow me to fill you in on a little secret, although I'm sure you probably already know it: your patience will be tested more than just about any other parent. Strong-willed children are a challenge all their own, and the battles that you face will be unique to you. There is no sense comparing yourself or your parenting method to your neighbor or friend from church, since their kid is completely different and most likely does not test his or her parents every single day like your child does. Admitting it is the first step, because only by acknowledging the difficulty in your own parenting journey can you allow yourself some breathing room in response to your own mistakes. And trust me, you will make plenty. We all do.

If there is one tip that you get out of this chapter on developing patience, it is remembering that your child is not the one making you angry—your perception to what is happening is what drives you up a wall. So many times, I get complaints from parents who tell me that their child "should" be acting in a certain way, or that this is how a kid is "supposed to" act. Who are you to judge that? Moreover, who gets to define what a kid should and shouldn't do?

We have this perception about children that they all sit straight-laced inside of a classroom and listen to the teacher, nodding their head and replying "yes ma'am" or "yes sir" to whatever the teacher says. Then, when they go home, they put their shoes by the door, change into their play clothes, and get started right away on their homework. I do not know about you, but that certainly wasn't the case in my house—even if it was the goal, ideally—and I highly doubt that is the case with most families.

The reason that you lose your patience with your child so often is because you have certain expectations that, quite frankly, aren't real. Your responsibility as an objective adult in this situation is to separate yourself from the way you think kids should be, and how your kid actually is. If you can remember this, life will be a lot easier in the long run.

Still, other parents swear up and down that their kid is out to get them. Like we talked about earlier, some parents honestly believe that their children have been sent here to torture them for some kind of past transgression, and as much as I try to convince them otherwise, they just entrench themselves further (and we wonder where the child gets their strong will!). Others think that a difficult child is a reflection of their own lack of parenting abilities, as if they were cursed from before time began to be a terrible parent.

Listen to me when I tell you that if you are reading this book right now, you are not a bad parent. A bad parent is somebody who does not care about their child, somebody who is disinterested and apathetic to their child's development. The fact that you are actively reading a book right now about how to become a better parent and teach your child, who may be difficult to deal with, is an indication that you care, and that is the mark of a good parent.

Before we can ever hope to develop patience within ourselves for how our kids are acting, you must be willing to cut yourself some slack. It's tempting to begin to look at ourselves whenever we see no logical answer for the reason our kids are the way they are, but the truth is never as simple as that. Be objective, look at the situation plainly, and develop a rational response to difficult situations when you feel your temper start to flare.

Following are a few coping strategies I recommend to everybody I come into contact with, and they may help you as well. Remember, the absolute worst thing you can do when you are at the end of your rope is to lash out at your child, so one way or the other, you must develop the ability to push your emotions down in a formal logical response.

- *Fight the Negative Thoughts.* You name them, I have heard them. People tell me all sorts of crazy things that run through their mind whenever their child starts to stubbornly resist any form of authority, from believing that other parents were judging their parenting, to honestly thinking that their child will end up in prison. Whether or not those two events are happening—or ever will happen—is completely irrelevant now; the only thing that matters in the moment is handling the immediate situation. Let's face it, you don't have the time or the energy to start thinking about the future whenever your child stomps his feet in the doorway and refuses to go to bed. You may think about those later, but now is not the time. Fight the negative thoughts and save those battles for another day, because in all honesty, they are not real anyways.

- *Look for the Practical Explanations.* My wife and I had a saying when our kids were little: food solves everything. I can't tell you how many times one of our kids would be crying and crying and crying, and we would try everything under the sun to try and get them to sleep—changing diapers, rocking, going on car rides, etc.—and nothing would work. However, 99 times out of 100, as soon as we fed them, they would go right to sleep. You may be thinking to yourself, "Well of course that is the case, you Dumbo!" but it was never that simple for us. It will not be that simple for you, either. When your child is putting you through the fight of your life, ask yourself if there could be some other reason they are acting the way that they are. Maybe they skipped their nap? Maybe they missed a snack? Maybe their sibling called them a name earlier that you did

71

not hear? Regardless, it is worth investigating other causes to see if you can solve the issue.

- *Eliminate Your Own Stresses.* Honestly, it is no wonder why some parents respond the way they do whenever I hear what they do for a living. One of my clients worked in a high-stress job as a defense contractor, putting in over sixty hours a week at the job, dealing with billion-dollar contracts on a regular basis. What do you think they were like when they got home? How could you possibly maintain your cool when you are under that kind of pressure all day long? You may not have the same level of stress at your job, but things like getting enough sleep, eating the right type of food, exercising, and having strong support systems in your life are extremely important to managing your own stress levels. If you do not have a way to balance the stress in your life, you can expect that your child will both realize it and feed off of it as they struggle to gain control in your household.

- *Remember: No Kid is Perfect.* Seriously, do not ever forget that. No kid, no matter how many great pictures their parents post on Facebook and Instagram, is ever perfect. I guarantee you that every golden child you see on your kid's baseball team has had at least fifty meltdowns in the last month that have caused their parents to sit and cry. Your kid is the same way, so if you get downtrodden about the way they are behaving, just remember that it is completely normal. Cut yourself some slack, you're doing a great job.

As much as we try to control our emotions in the moment, we still have to ask ourselves what we should do if we ever lose our patience. If you do retaliate or escalate the situation, remember that the way you respond is not science—it is an *A.R.T.*

Admit that you blew your cool. Before you ever try to explain away your behavior with your child, walk up to them and acknowledge that you lost your temper. You may not think they realize what you are doing, but I guarantee you that kids understand when you get on their level and apologize. Not only does it diffuse the situation, but it sets a great example for how they should handle conflict in their own lives.

Relocate yourself away from the situation immediately. My son wasn't more than three weeks old when I got the maddest that I had ever been toward him (and, honestly, ever would be). I was a new, first-time parent, sleep-deprived, and stressed trying to handle a baby that wouldn't stop crying. No matter what I tried, I could not find any way to make him happy—not even food! I could feel my hands start to shake and sweat begin to pool in my armpits. I knew that I had to leave the room, so I gently put him down—still screaming— and went to the other room and pushed against the walls as hard as I could. Whatever you must do in the situation to prevent it from getting any worse, do it. Don't argue and do not let your ego get the best of you; just leave. Give yourself some time to think.

Take charge of the situation. When you come back, get to work fixing what went wrong. If you said something you shouldn't have, apologize. If you broke your promise, keep it. If you need to get some late-night snuggles in, do that too. Clean up your mess immediately, and do not let the sun go down while you are still angry.

It is hard to overstate just how important it is to maintain your patience in times like this. When you are staring down the barrel of a strong-willed child, everything in the world slows down to see how you respond. And how you respond dictates everything. Take a few seconds to get your thoughts about you, maintain your objectivity, and do what needs to be done.

Chapter 12: Should I Discipline My Strong-Willed Child?

The topic of discipline can be sticky for most parents. While just about everybody agrees that at least some discipline needs to take place, the question of when, why, and especially how, can change from person to person. Most people are reluctant to talk about it just because of how contentious the issue can be, but like it or not, it needs to be discussed, especially when dealing with a strong-willed child.

Kids that are naturally defiant respond to a different set of incentives than other kids. Whereas some may be reward-motivated, for others, the thought of getting rewarded or not doesn't even phase them. Ultimately, what drives a strong-willed child more than anything, at least in terms of punishment, is the parent's attention. As long as they have your eyes, they are happy.

For some, this has led to speculation as to whether or not children become defiant precisely because they are deprived of this attention initially. I *strongly* disagree with this notion; I've seen kids from all walks of life and with every different type of parent under the sun express similar behaviors, so condemning the parents outright for the behavior of their child is not only incorrect, but dangerous. Unfortunately, that does not stop the rumors from circulating, and it does not stop the parents from feeling like they failed in some way.

All children act out because they want attention, but strong-willed children may require it more than others. How else are they to assert their dominance? How else will they get their way? The ability to tell you now—and, most importantly, do what they want to do—comes through resistance to your will.

Regardless of what type of discipline you eventually decide on for your child, one thing is clear: every negative action requires a consequence of some kind. Unless there is some kind of incentive for them not to act in the way that they are, they will continue to behave in a certain manner until they see that it doesn't benefit them any longer. Empty threats and broken punishments only embolden the child, teaching them that they can act however they want and everybody else will just deal with it.

By the same token, they should expect to receive a positive reward for doing something good, but humans are much more likely to respond to a negative behavior than they are to praise a positive behavior. Think about your own parenting life: When was the last time you actually praised your child? If it was recent, that's great, because a lot of parents—especially those with strong-willed children—are so tired of the negative behavior that they completely overlook the positive behavior.

We do not reward the positive actions nearly as much as we should, precisely because that is what we expect them to do in the first place. Why should I praise them for doing exactly what I have asked them to do?

Children respond directly to the consequences of their choices, whether good or bad. Positive reinforcement is critical for all kids, and in another chapter, we'll talk about how positive reinforcement can have a compounding effect on your child. You may not notice it at first, but over time, you'll see that your kid acquires a more positive and hopeful outlook, ultimately listening to you because they want to, instead of because they are afraid of what might happen.

The downside of constant negative reinforcement is that the dial consistently has to be turned up. What works as a punishment one day does not always work the next day; they got used to it, after all, so why should they fear it now? For some, this leads to an especially abusive form of corporal punishment, and if not, at least emotional punishment.

The idea is to create a balance of both discipline and reward, negative and positive consequences for their actions. To answer the question that is contained in the title of this chapter then, yes, you absolutely should discipline your strong-willed child.

But how are you supposed to do that?

For starters, pick your battles. It's easy to react negatively to every single thing that your child does, whether it is whining or moving slower than normal out of defiance. And while those certainly may merit some form of punishment, you must leave room for the larger punishment that comes from real problem issues, such as not listening to people who are in authority and encouraging others to do the same. These issues need to be handled so that your child can recognize the difference between something that is annoying and behavior that absolutely needs to stop.

Can you reason with them? I have had a number of well-meaning parents both ask me this question personally and display it in their interactions with their child. I have seen parents get on one knee and talk for at least twenty minutes to their child about what they did, why it was wrong, and why they should never do it again. I applaud these parents for having such a hands-on approach with their child, but in my experience, these types of conversations rarely reap results.

When the child is older, such as approaching six or seven years old, this is vital, but a three- or four-year-old usually does not have the patience to comprehend what the parent is saying. You must be direct and clear with them; concise conversations almost always win the day.

Reasoning with them usually does not work with strong-willed children precisely because you are giving them exactly what they wanted all along - your undivided attention.

Once the child can get your eyes and your focus, they win, and ultimately will do whatever it takes to retain that attention, even if that means reacting negatively. Such is another reason why concise conversations work better—you tell them what is going on, and you move on. Rewarding them with a long conversation can do nothing more than encourage negative behavior.

Does that mean that we should never talk to our child? Absolutely not! What I am saying though is that you need to be specific with your words, instead of dragging the conversation out for several minutes. Tell them what they did, why what they did was wrong, and the consequence for the wrong behavior in a few sentences, if you can. Keep it short, if for nothing else than your own sanity.

One punishment that I have noticed works tremendously for many parents is a timeout. It works especially well on strong-willed children, because in removing all distractions from their immediate area, you force them to sit and think about things, rather than constantly trying to engage. It is also relatively painless—for both you and the child. It may take a while to get the child used to receiving this type of punishment, but the earlier you can instill it as an expected outcome of negative behavior, the better.

Like every other part of your behavior, it needs to be consistent. Try to send them to the exact same place for their timeout every single time, whether that is a corner, a room, or even just on a couch. Make sure that there is nothing nearby that they can get in trouble with; bathrooms, for instance, pose several dangers that are all too alluring for a bored child. Make it somewhere that you can keep your eye on them so that they don't run off, and don't be afraid if they get imaginative while in timeout. Making their fingers walk on the floor, for instance, helps build the creativity part of their brain, and while it shouldn't necessarily be encouraged, it does not need to be reprimanded.

However long you decide to make the punishment, make sure that they understand that they need to be quiet for a certain period of time before they can come out of timeout. This includes noises made with their mouth, tapping on the floor, and anything else they can do to be obnoxious. The idea is for them to understand that when they create negative actions, they should expect to be isolated and bored—two things that strong-willed children absolutely hate.

As mentioned earlier, discipline can be tough for every parent. None of us, after all, enjoy watching our child in any kind of pain whatsoever, especially when it is completely avoidable. Unfortunately, parents that refuse to discipline their child for anything wrong almost always end up creating larger problems for themselves and everybody else that interacts with the child in the future. Don't think of it as a negative; think of it as crafting a character that will serve both them and others in the future. Your future self will thank you.

Chapter 13: How Your Kid Hears You

Strong-willed children are stubborn. You know that.

Strong-willed children also test your patience. You know that too.

And what you can deduce from both of those previous two statements is the fact that communication with your child is going to be different than the communication most parents have with their own children.

Let's not get too crazy, though—you're both still speaking the same language, after all. It's just that when you are dealing with a being whose entire existence is wrapped around putting up a fight and refusing commands at the drop of a hat, the form of communication you are going to take with them—at least in the beginning—is going to be much more direct and straightforward than it would be with others.

Humans communicate in four ways: verbal, nonverbal, visual cues, and writing. The key to communicating with your strong-willed child is that you leave as little room for misunderstanding as humanly possible, which is difficult for most parents. Most of us want to explain away every little reason why we do things, as well as convince or persuade our children to listen to us. We believe—mistakenly so—that by our many words, we are also heard.

With strong-willed children, this is simply not the case. Just as if you were in the middle of a legal battle with a room full of lawyers, anything you say can and will be used against you in the court of your living room. The child will latch onto every single word that you communicate, twist it, and then remind you of it days or even months into the future.

While some of these traits are common with many children, strong-willed children take this to an advanced level. They most likely will ignore you at first, but then, when you have their attention, they will zero in on what you have to say and look for loopholes. Did you mean that now? What actually classifies as cleaning your room? If I only eat some of my dinner, does that mean I can get down from the table?

It would be impossible to manufacture the right words in every scenario; moreover, doing so would drive you absolutely insane. But what I do want you to do is—at least for the next several months—focus on what you are saying and try to be as concise as humanly possible. Your goal is to be direct, clear, and understood. Sounds easy enough, does it not?

Unfortunately, there are a bunch of ways to very innocently mess this up, some of which are outlined below. Let's take a standard example of a parent who wants the child to clean their room. While the idea may be simple enough, the execution may not pass muster. If you want the room spotless, do not do the following:

Do Not String Together Commands

The first thing that I hear parents doing a lot is stringing together a bunch of instructions in a single sentence. If you have a to-do list for your child that consists of cleaning their room, but also putting away their clothes, and then brushing their teeth, many parents will try to put this in the same sentence to save time. Read it quickly out loud and see what you think. Unfortunately, all this really does is confuse the child. They most likely will not remember every single thing you told them, which will inevitably result in anger from the parent toward the child, which produces bitterness. If this chain happens several times in a day, you can see how antagonism can be built up over a few years.

Instead, do them one at a time. Look your child in the eye and very firmly, but gently, tell them to clean their room. Use as few words as possible, and wait for them to accomplish the task. If they try to fight or argue, simply restate the instruction and stand there as they move toward their room. By doing this, there will be no confusion as to what it is that you want them to do.

Do Not Ask a Question

In an attempt to soften the blow, I sometimes hear parents put the command in the form of a question. They may say, "Would you like to clean your room for mommy?" Without fail, the answer every single time is a firm "no."

Why do you think that is? It might go without saying, but if you are presented with the option to do something you don't want to do, you will most likely refuse it every single time. Think about it within your line of work: say your boss comes up to you and asks you, "Would you like to come in on the weekend to finish up those reports before the presentation on Monday?" Your response will almost always be a no. Why would it be any different with your child?

Do Not Be Vague

Using our example of a parent asking a child to clean their room, it might be better to tell them exactly what you expect them to do instead of simply making it "clean." Tell them to put the clothes in the dresser, the toys in the toy box, make the bed, and straighten the bookshelf. Instead of issuing an arbitrary command, you have very clearly laid out what you expect of them.

82

Instructions like "be good" or "be nice" are well-meaning but are so completely arbitrary that they can mean one hundred different things to one hundred different children. What one child may feel is nice may not be anybody else's definition, and yet in their mind, they fulfilled the request that was asked of them. Then, when you asked them why they weren't nice, they will respond that they were. An argument is soon to follow.

The most heartbreaking aspect of this error in communication is that the child honestly feels like they did what was asked of them, and so they do not understand why they are now in trouble. The parent, on the other hand, felt like they were specific enough; after all, who doesn't know what it means to genuinely "be nice" or make a room "clean"?

Children interpret things completely differently than the way you or I would, mostly because they don't have years of life experience to build on. You cannot expect them to navigate the emotional and social pitfalls of life without any foundation to back it up, no matter how advanced you may think they are. The absolute best thing to do in this situation is to be very specific with what you want them to do. If you want them to share their toys, ask them to share their toys. If you want them to stay at their desk, tell them to stay at their desk. Do not be vague, and you will not have to deal with a confused—and probably angry—child nearly as often.

Do Not Include the Reason

Yet again, we need to reemphasize the point that you should not reason with your child unless it is absolutely necessary, with a caveat for older kids who are able to understand clearer what you are asking of them. If you are dealing with the three- or four-year-old, however, you do not necessarily need to include the reason why you asked him to

83

do something at that point in time, no matter how much they ask for it. Nine times out of ten, they do not really care what the reason is, they are just stalling for time. In the event that you do give them a reason, they will begin an endless debate with you as to the merits of your reasoning, as well as possible alternatives that can achieve—in their mind, at least—a very suitable outcome.

In the same way that not being direct opens a multitude of pathways for them to fight you on, so does including a reason within your command give them room for arguments. And whatever you do, avoid the pitfall of simply saying "I told you so." For a child predisposed to fight against any form of authority, all that is going to do is give them rocket fuel to fight you every step of the way. If you don't believe me, just try it once and see how it works. You probably will not do it again.

These are certainly not the only things that could possibly go wrong with communicating to your child, but they are definitely the most common. Time and time again, I have seen parents try to reason and argue with their child, in addition to giving them confusing and lengthy commands, only to wonder why it is that their instructions aren't being followed. Most of the time, the parents are completely flabbergasted, but once they realize what they are doing, the situation reverses itself pretty quickly. That does not mean that you will have a child that suddenly falls in lockstep behind you, but it does mean that you will begin to make some headway, which is all we really want as parents.

Some may argue with me on this, but I firmly believe that rewarding the child after they listen to you is vital. As we'll talk about in the next chapter, this does not always mean an extra piece of chocolate, but it does mean reinforcing the fact that they listened to you and that you are thankful for that. By positively reinforcing immediately after the command is followed, you will set yourself up for success the next time a situation like this comes around.

Can I say one more thing? Be patient. It is extremely easy, especially when a child seems like they just want to fight, to rationalize and restate commands repeatedly, but you have to resist this impulse. Ultimately, what you want to do is give the instruction, wait for them to comply, and then restate it if they do not listen. At this point, discipline may become necessary, but only if you are confident that they have heard what you have to say in the first place. If not, the punishment will not only be useless, but could be counterproductive.

By being patient, you will communicate to your child that the most important thing in this moment is that they listen to you, above anything else. If you can focus on one thing at a time, you will win more battles in the long run.

Chapter 14: The Compounding Effect of Positive Reinforcement

The parents of strong-willed children have a difficult job. While they may be raising children that have a remarkable work ethic and an incredible moral center, they also must handle someone who will stop at nothing to get their own way, at least in the early years. This creates a ton of issues, and it can also foster a very negative relationship between the parent and child if the matter is not handled appropriately.

For that reason, positive reinforcement is so critical to develop early on. For the child, it may seem like everything they do gets shot down or refuted by the person that is in charge, whereas the parent may feel like the child simply doesn't want to listen to them. Neither of those things is true. Your child may not realize this, but as a parent, you must remember that most of these issues are the result of a simple misunderstanding, and with a little bit of work, a lot of the communication issues that we talked about in the previous chapter can be remedied.

One thing you can do, in the meantime, is create a system of positive reinforcement for your child. This is going to be very difficult in the beginning, mostly because it may feel like nothing your child does deserves to be rewarded. I guarantee you though, if you look hard enough, you will find various things that are worth praising your child for. It does not necessarily have to be big; in fact, something as simple as putting their plate in the sink may be worthy of a high five or a pat on the back. Any way that you can identify and reinforce your child's positive behavior is worth the effort. At the very least, in those moments when you are going toe-to-toe, they will understand that you have their back.

Creating a system of positive reinforcement also helps establish a baseline for you and your child as to what you expect of them. Some children honestly do not know what their parents want from them, and so they float, doing one hundred different things in hopes that the parent will notice them, whether positively or negatively. By isolating an individual behavior, no matter how small, and then praising them for it, you start to lay a foundation that they can build on.

In my experience, praising a child works best when it is done with specificity. Instead of simply saying "good job!" to your child, try to specify exactly what it was they did that was so great. For instance, you can say "good job putting your plate by the sink!" That slight change helps them to identify what specific type of behavior you are rewarding, and will most likely result in them repeating that action in the future.

Almost always, when I tell a parent to create a system of positive reinforcement, they want to know exactly how to do that. For some, they categorize positive reinforcement with some kind of physical or financial reward system; that is not entirely false, but it is also not totally true either. Positive reinforcement can come in a variety of different ways, but it always must be intentional. This will be difficult in the beginning, especially as you are more likely to notice all the negative things that they are doing instead of the positive, but as long as you put forth the effort, you will also notice the good things they do regularly.

If you are struggling to find ideas of how to reward your child, below is a list of things that I recommend to everyone I come into contact with, many of which have been tested in the real world to various degrees of success:

- *Verbal Compliments.* This is probably the easiest to accomplish, provided it is done with a measure of specificity. It is not enough to just say that they did something good, you must also tell them exactly what good they did. If you want to take it up another notch, tell them why it was so good.

- *Physical Touch.* It is often repeated inside parenting circles that every child needs at least seven physical touches a day to feel the love of their parents. While that number can be debated up or down, there is no doubt that kids crave physical affection from the parents. The research on this is endless. Certain studies have shown, for instance, the children who are coddled and held as babies sleep better, eat healthier, and are overall much happier than their non-held counterparts. With a toddler, you can accomplish a similar purpose by patting them on the back, giving them a high five, or giving them a long hug to show approval.

- *Activity Rewards.* One other popular form of rewarding a child is letting them do an activity that they love. This is where monitored screen time can come in very handy, but only if devices are not used all the time to begin with. If your child always has a pad in front of them, then an extra twenty minutes of screen time will not really matter that much to them. You could also let them play a video game, read their favorite story, or even go to the park. Activity rewards can also be one of the most potent forms of positive reinforcement, since the child immediately connects what they are receiving with the behavior that is being rewarded in the first place.

We can't talk about rewarding your child and creating a system of positive reinforcement without addressing some of the concerns that parents have. When I tell parents that they should reward their children for good behavior, a few of them will respond by telling me that doing so is a form of manipulation or bribery. They claim that by giving them a reward for positive behavior, I'm training them like I would train my dog, which, in their eyes, is demeaning.

I vehemently reject that argument, and have no trouble doing so in person. By creating a system of positive reinforcement, I'm ultimately communicating to my child that the desired activity is one that I want them to continue doing. In many cases, this is for their own personal benefit; listening to me is the precursor to listening to other authority figures, such as a teacher. Likewise, by eliminating the negative behaviors and encouraging the positive, I'm helping to guide my child down the ideal pathway and crafting a self-sufficient, well-rounded, and respectable member of society.

In other words, I'm being a parent.

I'm not saying that you need to reward every minor behavior with a trip to the zoo, but when a child does something good, they deserve to hear approval from you. Most of the time, that is exactly why these children do it in the first place—to elicit a reaction from you. Wouldn't you much rather have positive actions reinforced by positive rewards, rather than negative?

Once again, think about it in terms of your own workplace. Do you feel manipulated when your boss rewards you with a bonus because you closed an important business deal? If you are a teacher, and you were rewarded with better equipment to use in your classroom because your kids' grades were the highest in the school, would you feel demeaned as a result?

I understand why parents feel this way, but the truth is, children are not being manipulated or misled in any way. They are just being taught what to do.

It may sound silly, but as the parent, you must also be careful not to reward negative behavior. This happens by praising good behavior that is only partially good, or by praising the action even though they do it with a bad attitude. For the positive reinforcement to be effective, it must be completely wholistic. In other words, the entire event needs to be worthy of praise, rather than just a few parts here and there. If they do only a little bit of what they are asked, praise them specifically for that, but also remind them that they did not fully do what they were asked. Trust that they will be able to understand this point when it is made directly.

Children will want to get your attention one way or the other, and strong-willed children are no different. By creating a system of positive reinforcement, what you are doing is creating an environment by which it can be accomplished safely, without any fear of failure. It also creates a happier home. Who doesn't want that?

Chapter 15: Why Playing with Your Child Is Important

If life progresses as it normally does, your children are not going anywhere anytime soon. That is a good thing, despite the fact that children also have the capacity to make you lose sleep, pull out your hair, and create words that you never knew existed until you became a parent.

Along with those times when you feel like you are about to completely lose it, there are also moments that a parent truly feels absolute joy in what they are doing. They marvel as their kids grow and learn about the world around them, interact with friends, and seem to know just when you need a cuddle session the most. It is one of the many superpowers that every parent gets to enjoy on a fairly regular basis.

One of the things I have always loved doing is watching my children play. I remember one time, during an especially long car trip, where a stray napkin from a fast-food meal hours earlier found its way into the backseat. My oldest son—four at the time—picked it up, showed it to his little sister, and they then proceeded to play with it for the next two hours using just their imagination. They wore it as a hat, folded it up as a baseball to throw at each other, and even made a tiny finger puppet out of it for a few minutes. Hearing their giggles from the backseat is one of my favorite memories of them when they were little, and it is one that I will cherish for the rest of my life.

But even better than watching them play, is playing right alongside with them. Many parents are reluctant to do this, eager to scoop up those few precious moments where their children are occupied and they can have some peace. They feel like those moments when their kids are in the bedrooms playing amongst themselves are gifts directly from God Himself, and so they open their phone and scroll mindlessly through Facebook to let their brain rest.

There is absolutely nothing in the world wrong with that. Do not think for one second that I wrote this chapter to shame parents who seize opportunities to take some time for themselves. In contrast, the reason I wrote this chapter is to reveal opportunities they may not have noticed before to interact with their child. Parents of strong-willed children struggle with this the most, since strong-willed kids will push their parents' buttons almost constantly. Eager to attain their attention, they are rarely out of sight, and even more rarely, out of mind.

But every once in a while, I beg of you, when your child is playing in the back room by themselves or with siblings, wander into their room and just sit on the floor and watch them. Do not interrupt them (if it can be avoided), and just observe their minds at work. Even if they never acknowledge your presence, I guarantee you, you will walk away with a newfound appreciation for their presence in your life. And for parents of strong-willed children, that little reminder may be just what the doctor ordered.

If you do get the urge to play with your children, I would give you a word of warning: play with your children, instead of forcing them to play with you. The world of a child is imaginative, and more vibrant and colorful than adults can imagine. They create entire scenes and characters out of nothing, harvesting an entire universe from virtually nothing.

The flip side of this is they also have very strict and well-crafted ideas about how they feel this world should behave. If a parent comes in and demands they do something different, you may not only be rejected, but you may find them rejecting the playtime that is so fundamental to their growth. You are a guest in their world, and they will expect you to act like it.

Let's lay out some ground rules for play time with your children. This will not apply to every scenario under the sun; surely, there will be moments where you must force them to act in a different way for their own safety. But by and large, when you go into your child's world—wherever that may be— here are some things to remember:

- *Observe First.* Many parents make the mistake of coming into a play area and trying to "make the scene better." Inevitably, what happens is the child lashes out at the parent and tells them that is not at all the way their toys should be played with, or that it would be "better" for them to play a different way. What seems "better" to you may be horrific to them, so the very first thing you need to do is watch what they are doing. Get a feel for how they handle the characters, watch how they build the world, and see what the scene is setting up. This may sound like a lot, but it can be accomplished in less than a minute by just simply watching your children. It is imperative that you understand the world they are playing in before you enter it.

- *Ask for Permission.* Honestly, not every kid will want their parent to play with them all the time (parents of teenagers know this firsthand). Instead of just picking up an action figure and trying to play along, ask your child if you can play with them. If they say yes, ask them what character you can play with and what they want you to do with it. If they say no, just say "fine", and sit back and watch a little longer. They may change their mind in a few minutes, but even if they don't, at least we'll get some time to observe and enjoy.

• *Encourage Always.* Remember, whatever world they are building or whatever they are engaged in at the moment—that is everything to them. Use the opportunity to encourage them and point out specifically what you loved about what they are doing. This does not need to be nearly as robotic as it may sound; simply pointing out that an action figure jumped off the roof and did a high dive may be worthy of a pat on the back. Or if you did actually notice something that was amazing, point it out to them. Chances are, they didn't even notice it themselves. Once they know that you're there to have fun with them, instead of walking in and bossing them around, they will be much more apt to play with you in the future.

• *Leave Your Phone Outside.* It should go without saying, but this is not a time for you to have your mind engaged in anything else. If you carry your phone in with you, especially if you are a self-proclaimed phone addict, your child will recognize it as an intrusion into their world and will usually shut down. Leave your phone out of sight so you cannot interact with it, not even to take pictures. If you simply can't resist the urge to capture those precious moments, ask them for permission first and then retrieve it from the other room. The absolute worst thing you can do is intrude into their world and act completely disinterested. This will do nothing but discourage them and could ruin future play sessions.

Whenever I broach the subject of intentional play with a child, especially from an observer's perspective, I usually get a little kickback. Parents that don't understand the value of unstructured free time in their child's life will inevitably question why they should make this a focal point in their day-to-day life. I always point out to them that in doing so, you are creating a bond with your child outside the realm of normal parental behaviors, such as giving them instructions, asking them to eat their vegetables, or making sure they go to bed on time. You are creating a friendship, which should never come above your role as a parent, but can be invaluable to developing a healthy relationship in the long run.

It also helps with behavioral issues. As it is with every relationship, you cannot expect to influence them for the better if there is not a mutual love and trust present. By humbly entering their space and being a participator rather than the dominant force, you're allowing them—the strong-willed child—to be the one in charge. Kids love this, and best of all, it is completely safe for everyone when it is done in a structured environment.

With any luck, they will not only ask you to play with them again but may even begin to ask you for your opinion on how the scene should unfold. They might start to imitate your behavior and allow you to take the lead in certain scenarios, which will inevitably bleed over into other parts of your life with them. Once this happens, your relationship with them will be solid, and you will start to notice behavioral changes happening in other parts of their life. They may be more open to your instructions and more willing to bend to your rules, but will ultimately be friendlier overall.

This is when your relationship with your child can become truly beautiful. Not because they are mindless robots that bend to your every instruction, but because you have gained a friend for life that loves you and respects you and wants to do what is best for you and the rest the family, instead of just for themselves. This is ultimately what every family member should strive for—to put others before themselves.

You may not think that changes like this happen in structured playtime, but I have seen it time and time again with parents I interact with, and I assure you, it is a better use of your time than spending another hour of your life scrolling through social media, which, let's face it, we are all guilty of doing more than we should.

Chapter 16: How (and Why) to Completely Ignore Your Child

It may be weird to have a chapter devoted to ignoring your child right after a chapter that talks about the necessity of playing and interacting with them, but you must have a good balance when you are dealing with strong-willed children.

There will be times where you need to have fun with your children and give them all the attention in the world, and there will be other times you will have to ignore them completely for their own benefit. This is never done out of malice or anger, but for the simple reason that you cannot reward behavior that is not acceptable. And when attention is what strong-willed children crave, taking that away from them is one of the fastest ways to let them know what they are doing will not be tolerated—by you, or anyone else that may come into their life.

Before we go any further though, it is worth mentioning that there are a few times where you absolutely should not ignore your children. The first, and most obvious, is when they are doing something which can endanger their lives. If your child is jumping on the couch right next to a massive glass coffee table, then it is in everyone's best interest—including your child's—to tell them to get off the couch. The same goes for when they are playing on the playground in a hazardous manner, playing dangerous games with other children, or wandering into an area that poses risks. Those are not times that you should ignore your children.

Neither are times when they are completely disobeying you. If you told your child to do something once and they refuse to do it, engage with them so far as the mode of discipline that you have selected requires. They need to know directly, in those situations, what they are doing is unacceptable and needs to stop. Compliance with your instructions is paramount.

So, when should you ignore them? Mostly, when they are doing behaviors that are not necessarily disobedient and not dangerous, but are especially annoying and designed solely to get your attention. Whining fits, tantrums, any pleas that are strictly attention-oriented can be—and should be—ignored outright, or as much as possible. You may have to intervene at some point in the future but put forth strong effort to not even look at your child when they are engaged in these types of activities.

Why? Because if they do these things, and then you turn to look at them, they will know that is one of the ways they can get your attention. The next time a situation arises where they don't feel like you are listening to them, you can expect to hear the exact same type of behavior happening again, whether you meant to ignore them or not.

Ultimately, though, it is not about your own personal sanity. It is about teaching them there are ways you can get noticed that are not destructive, annoying, or damaging to relationships. To do this, inform them after they are done whining that these actions are not the ways to get your attention. Instead, encourage them to ask politely or wait for an opportunity that will not intrude on other people.

My kids were the worst at interrupting people in the middle of a sentence to ask for something, and I know the same is true of other kids. Ignore them for as long as is necessary, then when the behavior has stopped, explain to them what is going on.

If it seems like we are breaking every rule in the playbook discussed so far, you are not entirely wrong. While I may have encouraged you not ever to try and reason with your child, unless in the most extreme circumstances, this is one situation where it is a great idea to explain the situation to them. In some situations, the child may not even know that what they are doing is being deliberately ignored in the first place; in that case, a simple explanation should suffice. Sometimes you may have to have the conversation a few times for them to understand it, but always make sure you do not reward the negative behavior, but rather that you will encourage them—and even reward them, occasionally—when they display the appropriate behavior.

The one thing that will be difficult when you are trying to stop this behavior is consistency. It is surprising how hard it is to ignore your child not just once, and not even twice, but on the tenth time that they try to get your attention through less-than-desirable means. It can happen so innocently too. Out of habit, you may respond to whining simply to make the noise go away, rather than objectively standing your ground and deliberately ignoring them. It will take conscious thought—as do most of the things in this book—but the earlier you can nip this in the bud, the better.

That being said, I understand this can be a real issue for many parents. We are conditioned—biologically, even—to respond to our children's voices. When those sounds are strikingly similar to our children's pleas for help, the natural systems inside of our body can kick into overdrive. Despite our best intentions, we find ourselves responding to undesirable behavior, even though we made a firm commitment to ignore it outright.

For that reason, do not get down if this doesn't go smoothly right away. This is a process, and it requires training you just as much as it requires training your child to get it right. I promise you though, they will eventually get it, so have faith that it will pay off over time.

Chapter 17: Teaching Your Child How to Listen

You may not realize it, but teaching your child to listen may be one of the most important things you ever do to help them in life. If you can get them to slow down, listen to another human being, and respond appropriately, you will be doing a lot better than most parents do when they raise their child—strong-willed or not.

But how do you get to the point where your child looks you in the eye and measures every word that comes out of your mouth? Unfortunately, there is no bulletproof method for making sure that 100% of the time, your child responds appropriately to you; but there are some things you can do to help teach your child to develop an active listening skill, which is a trait that many adults lack as well.

The best news is that it is far simpler than you may realize. It consists of two parts: modeling and evaluating. You walk the child through the process of active listening, and then ask them to do the same while you analyze what they did right and wrong. Be careful not to give overwhelmingly negative feedback, as that could result in your child getting disillusioned and giving up rather quickly. Praise more than you rebuke, and your child will begin to actually enjoy the experience.

As a side note, I'm a staunch believer in the fact that many children honestly want to please their parents. While they may also enjoy asserting their own dominance inside the household, as well as breaking a few rules now and then, ultimately most kids find enjoyment in gaining their parent's approval. When the parent does not necessarily give the approval as often as they like, it can lead to a whole host of behavioral issues, but I believe the root of everything is a desire for the parents' acceptance.

Developing an active listening skill—and more importantly, creating a tighter bond between parent and child—will result in your child wanting to grow and learn because they know that it pleases you. They will look for opportunities to make you happy, and may even remind you of how happy they make you every step of the way: "Does that make you happy?" or "Am I doing right Mommy?" Statements like these are invaluable for building trust, love, and respect between parent and child.

When you decide to teach your child any social skill, it is imperative you not make it seem like a lesson. Instead, make them see it more as a game or a fun activity that you two can engage in. Do it informally, instead of setting something on your calendar every single week for fifteen minutes each. Make it impromptu so the child does not see it coming and it slips in naturally throughout the day. Try role-playing or make-believe and insert yourself and your child into real-life situations they will experience on an everyday basis. By using your imagination and making it fun, there is a greater chance your child will want to engage in this type of behavior with you, and most importantly, learn from it.

The process for teaching your child how to listen is relatively straightforward.

- *Teach them how to get your attention.* Kids will come up with all sorts of ways trying to get you to notice them, and as we talked about in the last chapter, not all of them are desirable. Help them to recognize that if they whine or throw a tantrum, it will not merit your attention; on the other hand, what does is politely asking for you to notice them or waiting for a break in the conversation. To demonstrate this in a real-life scenario such as an active listening game, do not let them talk until they recognize your attention is on them. If they try to talk when you are talking, turn and ignore them so they recognize the mistake.

• *Make them show you their eyes.* Great verbal communication relies on body language as much as it does the words that come out of our mouths, so make sure they know that you need to have their eyes. Do not put their head in a vise grip, obviously, but as soon as they take their eyes off you, stop what you are doing and wait for them to correct their gaze. Some kids will see this as an opportunity to practice their "creepy" face. While that may be funny, do not entertain it too much or else you'll be staring at those eyes every single time you try to have a conversation with them in the future. Trust me, I still deal with "creepy eyes" from my now adult children every once in a while.

• *Start short, and then make it longer.* When having these initial conversations where you are actively teaching them to listen to you, begin with short simple sentences and focus on keeping their attention squarely on you. The longer you draw out your sentences, the more likely they are to get restless and interrupt, or simply run off and ignore the rest of the lesson. Over time, you can allow yourself to elongate the sentences, or add more sentences to create an entire conversation where their attention is fixed on you, but at least in the initial phase, keep it short and sweet.

- *Compliment them when they are done.* Reward, reward, reward. I cannot stress enough how important it is to reward appropriate behavior and ignore or even discipline negative behavior. We are creating a baseline for the way they should act in the future, and there is no way for them to know what you want unless you show it to them. If they make it through the entire conversation (or even a few sentences) without breaking eye contact or running away, then make sure you at least verbally compliment them on what they did. To take it even a step further, give them a hug or ruffle their hair. Kids love that.

- *Try it again.* Rome wasn't built in a day, and neither will be your child's listening skills. To reinforce this type of behavior, make sure you do this with them at least a few times a week. As mentioned earlier, it does not need to be a formal scenario—in fact, it is probably better that it is not formal. Instead, look for openings throughout the day where you can work with them, and then compliment them when they do a good job. To take it a step further, you can even have them watch you and your spouse or someone else engage in conversation that retains this type of focus and ask them to imitate it. Reward and compliment if they can pinpoint what each party did right.

I'll admit, this whole chapter may seem a little like overkill, but it is hard to overstate the necessity of learning important social skills like this when your children are young. For most children, they may pick this up as time goes on, but if we are being honest here, we all know adults who still have not mastered this art. At the very least, you will have a considerate child who knows how to engage with people their own age and those older than them, which is a skill that will pay for itself many times over.

And lest you think this is a practice that can be used only with this specific type of skill, it needs to be mentioned you can have the same activity with just about any other skill you want to teach your child as well, such as learning how to share, waiting patiently in a line, or anything else you can imagine. Repetition is the key, along with rewarding good behavior. Once your child gets used to these games, the sky is the limit.

Chapter 18: What About My Child's Self-Esteem?

With all this talk about ignoring our children, rewarding them for appropriate behavior, and teaching them how to listen, the concept of self-esteem can get lost in the shuffle. In reality though, that is the last thing we want to overlook, because having a child with great listening skills and awesome classroom behavior is virtually worthless unless the child actually believes in themselves.

For centuries, people have wondered what the secret is behind self-esteem. I'm no Aristotle, but in my experience, self-esteem usually results from a simple math equation:

Confidence + Priorities = Self-Esteem

Every child has their own unique things they are good at. Some are awesome at sports, others excel in the classroom, while others may be a social butterfly. Everyone has their own distinctive talents (and shortcomings), but what really determines a person's self-esteem is their own importance they put on those activities.

Someone who does exceptionally well at baseball, but honestly believes that academic intelligence is a vastly superior skill set may chafe at the suggestion they should go pro, or even that they should pursue a baseball scholarship. While they wouldn't necessarily view it as a waste of time, in their mind, they think there are more valuable ways they could spend their life.

What drives self-esteem even further down is the belief that they are not good at the things they feel are most important. For that reason, there must be a two-pronged approach to building self-esteem in everybody, but especially strong-willed children. They must have a proper understanding of what is most important—which can change from family to family—but also the reinforcement necessary to pursue those things. Developing this usually requires a hefty dose of listening from the parents so they can identify and support the activities they know are truly important for their child.

Now that you know what to do to build up self-esteem, there are some other things we should avoid as we embark on this process.

Do Not Focus Only on Their Strengths.

As mentioned earlier, what a child is good at may not necessarily be what they are the most interested in. A parent that insists their child follow the area they believe the child is strongest in—whether that is to receive a scholarship or move into a "more successful" career field—will usually encounter a massive amount of resistance, especially if they are dealing with a strong-willed child. As the parent pushes more and more, the child will dig in their heels and react negatively— and in some cases, even aggressively—to what their parents insist they must do. Before long, you've got a full-scale rebellion on your hands.

Instead, ask what they feel is most important for them. I have seen kids that demonstrate an incredible aptitude for theater, despite their parents' insistence that they focus on more STEM-related fields. While I understand the financial implications of those can vary wildly, at the end of the day, it does not really matter what the parent wants, since it is the child who must live their life. By actually listening to what the child says they want to do, and supporting them in that, you encourage them to be the most successful at whatever field they believe is most important for themselves and for the world around them.

Do Not Assume Your Child Knows How You Feel About Them.

In my dealings with parents, I rarely find someone who underestimates the support they are actually showing to their child. In most cases, the parent will swear up and down they encourage their children all the time, whether verbal, nonverbal, or by rewarding them in some way. Then, when I talk to the children, they tell me they never feel any form of positive reinforcement from their parents at all.

Which one should I believe? Fortunately, that is not really for me to decide, because if the parent feels like they are showing support while the child does not, then there is a miscommunication regardless of where the truth is. I always encourage the parent to never automatically assume they know where they stand with their child, but instead, constantly communicate with them to see where they are at and what they are struggling with, then show support more than they feel is necessary. Especially as your child is moving through these difficult stages of early childhood into the teenage years, that support will be more valuable than you ever realized.

In addition, I would encourage you to help the children learn how to praise themselves. Positive self-talk is vital to combat the negative voices they sometimes hear in their head. If you can teach your children how to appreciate their own accomplishments in life, you will find you are dealing with an overall happier child than you would otherwise.

Do Not Ignore Everyday Successes.

I know that life can be very routine oriented, and you think a B- on a piece of math homework may not be worthy to be hung on the fridge. I get it. But in that routine, we can all miss some vital moments that will contribute, over time, to your child's emotional growth. Pointing out even the most minute things and praising them where you feel it is necessary can reinforce the fact that, at the very least, they tried, and they did not give up when it would have been easier to just ignore the homework altogether.

As much as possible, try to limit the negative feedback as they form their own opinions about their life. You do not want a child coming home with the B- that they are genuinely proud of, only to find a parent thinks it is less than satisfactory. At the very least, they will get conflicting opinions about what is right and wrong and try to push themselves even harder to develop an unattainable standard. By praising them every day for even the simplest things, you let them know that hard work, respect, and the core values that matter most, are appreciated.

Do Not Decide Everything for Them.

Few things are more damaging to a child than a parent who tells them what to think every single day. I have been in the room with parent and child who have come to me with self-esteem issues, but then when I asked the child what it is they think may be causing it, the parent talks over them. I'll ask them again, only to receive a response from the parent, or watch as the parent rebukes the child for what they think is an incorrect answer. I then turn to look at the child, who almost always has a look of defeat on their face. No wonder they're in my office to begin with.

Listen to me very closely on this: Your child needs to learn to think on their own, even when you disagree with them. Unless it is a disagreement that throws them way off course or could result in physical danger, your job as a parent is not to decide every single thing for them, but to teach them how to make decisions. Allow them to take risks; while nerve-racking, this can help them establish confidence in what they decide to do and at the very least, they can learn to recover if something goes wrong. Your child needs to learn that no matter what they decide for their life, there is always a way to make it right. If you are deciding their life for them, then not only will they have no confidence in their own decision-making abilities, but they will be paralyzed by inaction as they try to determine their own future.

This does not mean you allow your children to completely go off the rails, but it does mean you should give them some leeway to make choices when you can. It is still your house, after all, but it is also their life. They should be the ones that learn how to live it.

Do Not Do Everything for Them.

I once dealt with a person in her early 20s who was wracked with self-doubt. I could not figure out what was causing her angst; on the surface, everything seemed great. She had a great job, great relationships, and was doing well in graduate school.

Once I dug a little deeper though, I found out that every single morning when she was in high school, her mom still did her makeup and her hair before she went off to school.

Then, when she got home, her father usually cut up her food for her before it came to her plate.

While these may seem like relatively minor things, added up altogether, they reinforce a belief that you are not capable of handling your life by yourself and that you will always need other people's help to succeed. Everyone, no matter the age, needs to learn to take ownership for their lives and for their attitude; otherwise, they will constantly be looking for other people to take care of them when they are capable to take care of themselves.

I encourage parents to give their children age-appropriate responsibilities and chores around the house, allowing them to learn how to approach problems on their own. Help them when it's necessary, but even if they come to you ten times in a row for help, encourage them to go back and handle the problem themselves. It is the only way they learn how to grow and how to develop self-confidence.

Do Not Be Overbearing.

There's no doubt about it; if a parent expects perfection from their kids, it is usually because they expect perfection from themselves. As anyone who has lived longer than ten seconds can tell you, we all make mistakes, so expecting your child to be perfect is insane. And yet, I still have parents who demand to know why their children are struggling in school, when the worst grade they have ever received is a B+ on a pop quiz.

The only thing overbearing parents are accomplishing is creating a child with severe anxiety issues and impossible standards that will give them a great deal of stress later in life. You are not perfect and your child is not either, but the strong-willed streak in them may convince you they are capable of it regardless. Reject this poisonous attitude with every fiber of your soul, and accept your children for who they are regardless of what you wish they would be, while always encouraging them to be better.

As mentioned above, it is nearly impossible to overstate just how important self-esteem is to a child. It is something to be cultivated, encouraged, and built up over time through micro-encounters with yourself and the others around you. You may not think you have as much of an influence on your child as you really do, but putting forth even just a little bit of effort every single day and fostering a child with good self-esteem will serve you, and them, in the long run.

Chapter 19: Nine Steps to Solving Just About Any Behavioral Problem

At this point, you should have a good foundation when it comes to understanding and interacting with your strong-willed child. That does not mean this book is perfect (nothing compares to real world experience, after all) but if you have made it this far, you are better prepared than most to tackle the challenges that come with having a strong-willed child.

That being said, I believe strongly that everybody should have a "pin-able" list of guidelines to go through whenever you are dealing with behavioral challenges. The depth and intensity of these issues can vary from person to person, but that does not make them any less important. Moreover, it is foolhardy to have a blanket approach to solving every single behavioral issue. It's far better to have a list of items in your toolbox that you can turn to depending on the situation.

Many of the suggestions in this chapter have been covered already in some detail, but it is good to have a refresher course on some of the highlights. I have thrown a lot of information at you in the last several pages, but these are the actionable tips—the bullet points of what you need to know. Think of this chapter as a summary of what we have already talked about. In fact, if I could recommend just one chapter for you to read—or if you were to give one chapter to one of your friends who is dealing with a strong-willed child—this is it. Aren't you glad I included it at the end?

Whether you are dealing with a child refusing to brush their teeth or a toddler having a full-blown meltdown in the middle of a grocery store, here are some things to work through as you approach virtually any behavioral problem that you will ever encounter.

Acknowledge the Problem

Strong-willed children thrive in getting your attention above anything else, so indulge them. Give them a few seconds of your attention, but not the kind of attention they're wanting (if they are doing it in a negative way).

Instead of giving in and hoping this situation will resolve itself, look them square in the eye and acknowledge what they are doing. Tell them, in a hushed but firm tone, what they are doing is unacceptable. Force them, through your gaze, to focus on you and listen to what you are acknowledging. Even better, get them to repeat what is it you said to them so you know they have heard it. If they do not repeat it after a couple times, locate them to a new position (if possible) and do it all over again until you are confident they have heard you.

Look for Outside Influences

What can be perceived as a simple meltdown usually has other factors at play, whether hunger, sleepiness, or maybe they just don't feel well. On one occasion, my child threw the fit-of-all-fits while sitting in his high-chair, refusing to eat green beans and chicken that I put on his plate (normally a big fan of both). The screaming went on for probably fifteen minutes as I tried to convince him to eat when, suddenly, I remembered the kid loves ketchup. A squirt later, and all of his food was in his stomach. I don't bring that up to tell you ketchup solves everything (although I would argue it solves most things), but as a gentle reminder to cover all your bases before you turn immediately to DEFCON three.

Address Any Anxieties

If your child is scared or nervous about something, the best course of action is to acknowledge it if you can. Fear in toddlers can come straight out of left field and can be as crippling as a panic attack would be in an adult. The last thing they want to do is have their fears invalidated, so make sure you acknowledge it and offer any alternatives or substitutions that may ease the process. If they refuse to go to bed, offer them a choice of staying up an extra five minutes in exchange for a more peaceful bedtime. Getting a little bit of their way now may lead to you getting all of your way later. Not to mention the fact that if you try to force them to go to bed, it could be a lot longer than five minutes before they actually comply.

Handle It as Quickly as Possible

Have you seen a parent that ignored their screaming child at a restaurant? I have too, and it is painful for everyone involved. While we did address the concept of ignoring your child in the earlier chapter, there is a difference between refusing to acknowledge mildly inappropriate behavior and just allowing your child to perform totally unacceptable behavior, especially in a public setting. In my experience, at least, children almost never go from completely silent to full-throttle screaming at the drop of a hat; rather, they almost always ramp up to it over the course of a few minutes.

If you detect that your child is on the verge of a meltdown—and most parents are familiar enough with their kid's whining patterns to know the difference—then intervene as quickly as possible to prevent it from turning into a scream fest. Once they get to that level, it's nearly impossible to bring them back down to earth, no matter what you try.

Model Good Behavior

In some cases, the child may genuinely be confused as to what it is they need to do. For that reason, you should try to model good behavior for them so they know exactly what is expected and, more importantly, how to do it. Showing them how to delicately get your attention is one such skill, as is waiting patiently in line, and learning where talking in a whisper is expected. All of these are important social skills that need to be developed over time, but the only way they will know is by watching you first. If your child is absolutely losing it, make an effort to model the good behavior so they will be encouraged to replace their own with what they see.

Ignore, if Possible

Whatever it takes, you absolutely do not want to give any encouragement to your child's poor behavior. If they do decide to act out in public, discipline them in such a way that they will be less incentivized to do it again.

In a restaurant situation, some parents will give their children a few sips of Coca-Cola or an extra helping of fries just to keep them quiet and make the situation slightly less embarrassing (hey, we have all been there). All this teaches the child is that if they want those treats later, they just need to act out. Ignoring the situation as much as possible lets them know it is not the way to get what they want. Showing them how to do it properly, as we mentioned in the last section, will help to stem the tide.

Discipline as Necessary

If you walk into any home in America, you will find a variety of disciplinary measures being enacted on children on a daily basis. Some people prefer timeouts, others retract rewards, while still some utilize groundings, provided their children are older.

Whatever your family decides is an appropriate punishment, make sure it is something that actually teaches them what they are doing is wrong, and is consistent no matter the scenario. You may not think children realize when their parents are being inconsistent with discipline, but the slightest misstep could cause them to call you out and put your integrity on trial. It is nearly impossible to back your way out of that. Make sure everyone in the family understands what punishment will happen to what crimes.

Be Patient with Them

We all have hard days, and strong-willed children seem to have them more often than others. If you are struggling with your child and constantly wondering when it is they will flip that switch and turn into somebody more agreeable, remember, be patient. Your child is learning just as other kids are, but they have certain psychological factors that make them more stubborn and resistant to external forces than others. The plus side of all this is that you are also developing a child that will be much more confident and independent in the future than other kids may be, at which point, you will wonder why you ever worried in the first place. I know it is nearly impossible to do so when you are in the thick of it, but try—for the sake of your child and your sanity—to be patient.

Praise Them When They Do What Is Right

It really doesn't matter if your child's good behavior comes after thirty minutes of a screaming fit, or if it is so minuscule you must watch them like a hawk in order to see it - make sure you double down on praise whenever you notice your child doing something good. They need to learn that negative behavior will be punished, but also that good behavior will be rewarded, and that it is in their own best interest to choose one over the other.

This will take more intentional thought than some of the other items in this list, but it is much more enjoyable for everyone involved. Even to this day I'm surprised by how powerful a high five and a pat on the back can be for a child's self-esteem.

In the moment dealing with your child's behavioral issues can feel like almost an impossible struggle, but if you move through the list above, piece by piece, you will have a much higher chance of success than if you react emotionally. While you never want to encourage your child's poor behavior, you also do not want to cripple them to the point where they cower in the corner and lash out whenever somebody approaches them. As parents, we are in the business of building children up, not tearing them down. May we never forget that.

Chapter 20: The Absolute Worst Thing You Can Do

We are fast approaching the end of our book on parenting strong-willed children, and my hope is we have been able to pick up some nuggets along the way. I realize not everything in this book will apply to every parent, and in fact, you may find yourself disagreeing with me out loud. That's okay. In all my years of working with families, I have gotten used to parents disagreeing with me on just about everything, whether it is discipline or reward systems. I can handle it.

What I do not want you to do is to simply throw this book away and operate purely based on instinct when it comes to the interactions with your child. As a parent or guardian, you are the number one influence in your child's life—for better, for worse—and it requires a game plan to craft them into the well-respected, well-rounded adult that we all hope they will be once they grow up.

But if there is one thing I have seen parents do over and over again that has the absolute worst effect on a child's self-esteem, self-confidence, and overall quality of life, it is this: dismissing the child's feelings, whether outright or through passive disinterest.

I sympathize with both parties when I see this happen. I sympathize with the parent because I know they are at the end of the rope, but I also sympathize with the child, because I know they feel like their voice is not heard. Strong-willed children are contentious by nature, and since very few people in this world actually enjoy conflict (besides the strong-willed children themselves, of course), the usual course of action is to shove it off until later and placate them in the moment.

You may feel like an absolute genius for quelling the immediate problem, but the failure to recognize and deal with your children's behavioral issues only makes it worse in the end. You will exchange a few moments of peace for a lifetime of misery, as the child continues to be unaware of what the exact behavior is that is causing problems. Later, once they are in school, they will be confused as to why the parent approves behavior at home while the teacher doesn't in the classroom. They also won't understand why the entire world doesn't stop once they start talking, and they will begin to get frustrated, angry, and possibly aggressive as a result.

Children need your trust and your respect more than just about anything else in this world. They also need to feel like they are valued members of the family unit. If we dismiss their issues out of hand, then we are telling them that neither of those things are taking place. As a result, they will start to look for validation, love, and trust in other places, and they will not always find it where you want them to.

At this point, you may be asking me how what I just said lines up with the earlier chapters that have to do with ignoring your child outright. The difference is twofold. For one, the chapter on ignoring your child only deals with ignoring unsavory types of behavior such as whining, temper tantrums, and other things that are not downright destructive, disobedient, or rebellious. Secondly, ignoring is a very calculated and deliberate move that does not communicate to your child you are dismissing them outright. Once they are done with their action, the responsibility is on you to then turn around, acknowledge what just took place, and remind them it is not acceptable.

By placating your child's poor behavior with the treat they did not deserve, or yelling at them while you scroll endlessly on your phone to block out the noise, the only thing you are communicating is that what they are saying is not as important as your own personal comfort. That is a dangerous proposition to make a child believe, and you can expect they will go to great lengths to get your attention one way or another.

A child's world is so small, and inside of that little world filled with make-believe, cartoons, and family, is a sense of self-importance that needs to grow over time. I have seen children with vastly inflated egos that believe they are the center of the universe, and while this can be dangerous, I would always err on the side of the child having too much confidence rather than not enough. When they do not feel like their voice is heard, they will try to show you why their voice needs to be heard.

When you dismiss them out of hand, you are also acknowledging defeat. You are telling the child you have essentially given up trying to help them, and they are completely on their own to handle their behavior from then on out. While everyone needs a break from time to time, you cannot afford to completely check out of your child's upbringing. Unfortunately, I have seen too many parents that have marched their three-year-old into my office and have told me they are utterly confused and do not know where to go from here. While I don't think any parent should throw their hands up in the air completely, three years old is just too young for a parent to be that confused.

At this point, allow me to restate something that I said very early on in this book. If you are reading this right now, and especially if you got this far, then know you are not giving

121

up. You are trying to be a better parent for your child that you love so much, and by seeking out valuable resources like this, you are telling your child their opinion does matter to you. When you check out and dismiss your child's behavioral issues though, it has the opposite effect. It shows them you have given up and their future is not nearly as important to you as whatever else it is you are doing at the time.

I have also seen parents begin to actually resent their children for their behavior. The parent begins to believe the children's behavior is unmanageable, and it is merely their lot in life to deal with disobedience and disrespect for the rest of their days. It is a very dark path to start down, and I would urge you to resist that temptation at all costs. It is vital that you maintain an optimistic outlook toward the future of your child, and that you always believe they are capable of so much more than whatever it is they are showing you in the moment. As Yoda would say, "Fear is the path to the dark side. Fear leads to anger. Anger leads to hate. Hate leads to suffering." You never want to be the Darth Vader in your family. Ever.

Finally, when you dismiss your children outright, you are signaling to them that you are not open to change. You are telling them you have your own way of doing things, and if they want to survive in this family, then they need to conform 100% to the way you do things.

Show me an organization of any kind that runs like that. Show me a business where the CEO has adopted the same mindset from the time they started their company to the time that they exited it. Show me an individual who begins a college education and does not grow and adapt to the everyday circumstances as they progress. Show me a person who is rigid in their behavior, and I'll show you a person who is cold, dark, and emotionally unavailable to those around them.

Being a parent means being open to change. Being a parent means you are open to wiping a dirty bottom in the middle the night when you would rather be sleeping. It means you give up your Thursday night Netflix marathon to coach your six-year-old's baseball game. But most of all, being a parent means you are open to giving and receiving love as a member of a family, whatever that may mean. If you insist your child dutifully responds to every single thing you say without any argument whatsoever, then you are not raising children anymore—you are raising robots.

It is so easy to dismiss a child's behavioral issues, thinking you will deal with them later. But the truth is, if you insist on pushing issues back farther and farther, then all you are doing is rolling up a snowball that will eventually come back down the mountain and crush you. It is far better—and easier—to handle a small problem today, than it is to delay the inevitable and deal with a mountain of problems later.

That is why dismissing a child's emotions is the absolute worst thing you can do to a strong-willed child. Not only does it affect them today, but it fundamentally changes the family unit and can greatly impact their future. Handle the issue now, no matter the cost.

Chapter 21: Dealing with the Strong-Willed Teenager

I know we have spent a great deal of time in this book talking about toddlers, but we could not end this book without talking at least a little bit about what to do if you are dealing with a strong-willed teenager. Hopefully, you're reading this book at a time when your children are still young and malleable, but I also know there may be some coming to this book later than others and are dealing with a 14-year-old who refuses to listen to anything that comes out of their parent's mouths, much less do what they say.

While that barrier may seem difficult, it is by no means insurmountable. From the moment your child enters your life to the moment they leave your home, you are the greatest influence they will ever have, only to be replaced by their own family later. Quite a bit of research has gone into how much your friends will impact you, and while that is true, no single person has as much impact on a child than a parent or guardian.

For that reason, I want you to know you are never too late to start implementing the guidelines in this book. While the specific suggestions may change—a temper tantrum can be replaced by a teenager slamming the door on the way to their bedroom, for example—the overall approach is the same: acknowledge, discipline, reward, and praise. The only difference is in how you apply them.

Unfortunately, I cannot give you a specific play-by-play of every behavioral issue that you will face as the parent of a strong-willed teenager, but that does not mean there is nothing to say on the topic.

First, I want you to realize just how difficult a job you have in front of you. I always sympathize with parents of strong-willed teenagers, not just because they are dealing with a tough personality now, but also because they have most likely been dealing with one for years. If you are staring into the eyes of a 13-year-old who refuses to budge on anything you tell them to do, I would imagine that is just another incident in a long line of things you two have had to deal with in your life together. That is painful, it is difficult, and I cannot imagine how emotionally exhausted you are.

I know my words may not bring you any comfort, but at the very least, you will hopefully be able to give yourself a little slack for what you are dealing with. You are to be applauded for the fact you are still seeking help after all these years and have not just completely given up. If you are seeking professional help with relationship issues between you and your child, then a double round of applause for you. It is absolutely vital that you try to take care of these relationships as quickly as possible. While I have never personally seen any children leave the house and become serial killers as a result of poor parenting, I have seen many teenagers walk out from underneath their parent's roof and have incredibly strained relationships for years to come. Those are formed, in large part, from the experiences they had living together, and they can last for decades.

That being said, it is never—ever—too late. Even if your children are out of the house and have refused to talk to you for months or even years at a time, you would be surprised how open they would be to re-engaging with you if they simply found a door that was open to them. In some cases, those doors need to be cracked ever so slightly by the parent swallowing a massive slice of humble pie. In others, a little persistence and self-sacrifice will do the trick. But regardless of where you are with your child, hear me out on this: it is never too late to repair a strained relationship.

Secondly, you should also realize the level of disrespect and rebellion will only rise as your children get older. Not only can they become more staunch in their opposition to you and refuse to listen to anything you have to say, but they may also be more strategic in what they do. They may conspire to pit one parent against the other parent, or twist your words to the point where you are confused as to what you actually said in the first place.

To help with this, you need to be intentional about your relationship building and in tune with your spouse as to what you two agree is acceptable underneath your roof. If you are going at it alone without the help of a partner, then, surprisingly, it gets slightly easier. Your child cannot try to play one parent against the other, and they cannot lean on what the other parent said in trying to convince you that you are wrong. Remember what you said, stick by your principles, and you will notice your strong-willed child will begin to crack a little under the pressure.

Whatever you do, do not give an inch if you see this type of manipulation taking place. It would be very easy to emotionally respond to your daughter pleading with you for the car keys to go to a concert seven towns away, but if you have already decided that—since it is a school night—they need to be in bed by 10:30, stand by that. Your child may not like it, but they will ultimately respect you as long as that rule is enforced consistently and fairly. In addition, you can also make a compromise: if they stay in tonight, you will let them stay out a little later on the weekends. This is a tactic we mentioned when we talked about dealing with toddlers and bedtime, but there is no reason that it cannot apply to teenagers as well.

Thirdly, do not be afraid to actually give them more independence if you feel comfortable with it. If your teenager is chafing against what they feel like is an undue burden placed on them by you, then go in the opposite direction. Let him stay out a little bit longer or let him take the car but remind him you are placing your trust in him to do what is right at the right time. You may not think a preemptive guilt trip could work, but you never know. Moreover, for especially strong-willed children, they may find a way to circumvent you anyway, which means that breaking your rules will actually give them joy, instead of sadness.

This is not to suggest that you just give your kids free rein to do whatever it is they want to do. On the contrary, you have already laid down the rules and the instructions for what they need to do, but now you are simply giving them the freedom to make their own decision. If you have taught them what to do and how to respond to various scenarios, you should be confident that somewhere deep down inside their psyche, they will make the right decision. And if they do not, they will also know you have their back.

Sometimes teamwork can be more important than strict disciplinary measures at this stage in the relationship. Like it or not, your teenager is quickly approaching the age where they will be forced to make their own decisions for their life. You will not be able to control them once they go off to college, or once they enter the workforce and live in their own place, but what you can control is your relationship with them and whether or not they feel like you trust them. Which will, in turn, make them trust you.

I remember one incident with a parent many years ago, who came to me for several months talking about repairing the relationship with his then 16-year-old daughter. She had a reputation as being a little bit of a loose cannon; he was worried that she would get into a situation she could not escape from, and he was determined to do everything he could to make sure she never got there in the first place. I reminded him that she would be leaving for college in two short years, and if he wasn't able to control her now, he certainly wasn't going to be able to control her once that happened.

"So what do I do, then?" He asked with a tender look on his face.

"Be her ally. Be her support team." I responded.

When I told him that, I didn't mean he needed to take a back seat to her life, but that he needed to reposition the way he felt he influenced her. Instead of being the authoritative dictator that could pick up his three-year-old daughter and put her in time out whenever he wanted, he needed to develop a relationship based on trust and support. Sure enough, a few months later, after he had integrated more of a teamwork mentality with his teenager, he told me she had gone to a party where, unexpectedly, alcohol was present. He told me that she did not drink, but she became nervous as she watched her friends slowly become inebriated. Because of the relationship and trust they built over the previous several weeks, she felt comfortable enough that she could call him to come get her, no questions asked.

I watched as the tears streamed down his cheeks. He told me it was the first time in a while that he felt she truly looked up to him as a parent and as somebody she could trust.

He told me how good it felt for her to look to him for help instead of her saying he was always trying to keep her under his thumb. Even though I have no doubt their relationship will experience more tense moments in the future, I have every confidence now that they are on the road to friendship as allies inside the family, rather than as combatants.

Just because your child is strong-willed does not mean they are a problem; in fact, this should be the time in their lives where you are starting to see independence and self-discipline come into full bloom. Most likely, you have a child at this point who is very sure of themselves and able to resist the peer pressure swarming them every single day. Instead of running from that, lean into it and embrace your child's rugged individualism, trying your best to hang on for the ride.

It'll be bumpy, but I guarantee you it will be worth it.

Chapter 22: How the Strong-Willed Child Changes YOU

We have talked a lot in this book about how to help the strong-willed child in their march through life. We have addressed certain behavioral issues, a few problem areas that need to be developed, as well as cultivating those independent streaks that are bound to happen. Along the way, you may have noticed there is a lot of hardship and stress in your future, but at least now you have a game plan with which to attack it.

What we have not really talked about is how the relationship between you and your strong-willed child affects *you*.

In my work dealing with families over the last several years, I can easily notice the transformation of the child. It is subtle, but usually there. Either the child will begin to show affection toward the parent, or they will start to listen and not interrupt as much, or they will just completely take off, embracing the relationship with their parent in a way neither I nor them thought was possible.

But inevitably, I always notice the parent has changed as well, and that is the part that sometimes brings a tear to my eye. To see someone go from complete hopelessness, thinking their child cannot be helped and is doomed for a lifetime of detention and jail time, and then transition into a person who is hopeful for their child's future, is a beautiful thing. Sometimes, once the child leaves the room, the parent will come back in and just give me a hug, thanking me for the work I have done with their children.

While I'm always quick to remind the parent it is them that did the work, I cannot help but be thankful for my own role in the process. As a counselor, I give them the tools to implement in their everyday life, but as the parent, it is their job to put those tools to work. When the process is allowed to develop, and the parent and the child both grow as a result, the effect is profound. The parent usually thinks it is the child that has changed the most, but in nearly every case, the more obvious transformation is the one the parent makes along the way.

I cannot guarantee you much in this book, but one thing is for sure: *You will be a different person at the end of this process than you were at the beginning.*

But how exactly will you change? That is the million-dollar question, is it not?

There is no doubt about it, the biggest change you will see inside yourself is that you will become a more patient individual than you ever thought you could be before. Parenting has a way of doing that to us anyway, but when you couple the parenting experience with a strong-willed child who wants to do nothing but fight back every step of the way, the effect is multiplied exponentially.

The fact that you cannot return a child, like you would something you buy in the store or even a car, forces the parent to deal with the situation as it is in front of them. As we discussed several times in this book, some parents simply shut down and hide their children, while others rise to the challenge and face it head on. I'm proud to say that, at least in my dealings with parents, most choose the latter option, since it is the way many people see has the most long-term success.

When they do, they are forced, by the very nature of the situation they are in, to be more patient. They cannot react

131

emotionally. They cannot just lash out. They also can't force their way through the problem. Instead, they must look it in the eye and deal with it—however long it takes.

As a result, you will also be stronger. You may find throughout your journey there are things that used to bother you a great deal that do not nearly have the impact on you they once did. For me, personally, the biggest change was in handling other people's kids. Once I saw my own strong-willed child and developed patience and strength in handling his issues, the negative reaction that I normally had toward other people's kids changed from anger to sympathy. When I heard a child cry in the store, I did not immediately get annoyed; instead, I stealthily moved in that direction if I thought I could be of some assistance. Nearly every time, I never said anything, but there was more than one occasion where I offered a knowing smile as a means of long-distance support. It was almost always returned.

That truly is one of the biggest benefits of being a part of the "strong-willed child" community. There are entire subcultures that revolve around parents of autistic children, dyslexic children, and special needs children; and while I absolutely would not put a strong-willed child in the same category as those by any means, there is a sense in which you can look at other parents dealing with similar struggles and form a connection. We have a tight bond among us that only we understand.

It is contingent upon you to find that community, but I guarantee you will not have to look too hard to find it. As I write this, I know of at least a couple Facebook groups, subreddits, and other online forums where people with strong-willed children gather on a regular basis to discuss certain challenges. You may find some issues they are dealing with that sound very similar to those we have talked about in this book, but you may also notice some completely off-the-wall scenarios that no one is prepared for, least of all the parent.

Inevitably, what you will also find in those tougher situations is a community that rallies around you. You will develop friends and allies you never knew you had, and also, never knew you needed. This stronger, more patient version of yourself now has a tribe that can carry you through this.

But you will not only find allies online or with other family members, you will also realize that your own strong-willed child—yes, the same one who throws a massive temper tantrum every night when you tell them to go to bed—will soon become your biggest fan. As parents, we cannot ever afford to forget that we need help too, and just as we are trying to help our children navigate this road through life, we are walking it ourselves. We pick them up when they fall, and in time, have faith that they will help pick you up as well.

It is hard for me to write this without feeling a little emotional about my own life. Ever since that fateful night years ago when Eric slammed his fist on the ground and refused to go to bed, I have prayed and wondered what kind of child he would turn in to. Now, I'm happy to say not only is he a well-respected member of society (at least, in my opinion), but he is also one of my very best friends. I do not say that because I must, but because I genuinely mean it. I love talking to him about life, asking him his opinion about things, and using him as a sounding board when I need it personally.

The strong-willed traits that I was angry about for so many years have now turned into qualities that I admire in Eric as an adult. He is disciplined, strong, determined in whatever he puts his mind to, and has a strong moral center that I sometimes wish I had. I have been known to waffle between opinions, but when I ask him what I should do, he gives me a very objective opinion that tends to clear things up quite a bit of the time. His influence in my life now is just as great, if not greater, than any influence I imagine I have ever had in his.

He has also forced me to be more open about various things. Before I knew him, I would have never thought there are seven different ways to squeeze toothpaste from a bottle, for instance. When Eric was a kid and I insisted he use the one I thought was normal, he reacted negatively. Why would you squeeze it from the center when it is much more fun to squeeze it directly on the counter and then wipe it on the toothbrush from there?

Even though the example is silly, the same point can be carried over to every facet of life. As Eric got older, I would argue with him about a specific point, and he would raise an objection I would have never thought of before, and yet found to be extremely valid. Instead of holding fast to my own opinion about the way things should go, I bent a little to his will, and in the process, learned a little something new myself.

It is this type of openness that I feel every parent, but especially those with strong-willed children, need in their lives. They need to bend a little, be more patient, be more forgiving, be more compassionate, and be willing to go outside their comfort zone to find support when they need it. In this way, I do not believe strong-willed children are a curse set upon us, but a blessing that allows us to get outside of our own way. You may disagree with me, and I know good and well the last place you will agree with me is when you are in the middle of a fight with your child. But trust me on this, *it will all be worth it.*

I cannot over-state this enough: given time, your strong-willed child will become a blessing to you. You never know when you may need their assistance to handle something or need their opinion when you are facing a tough decision. Even as I deal with my own parents and struggle to know what to do sometimes, my children's objectivity helps me to see the way. I lean on them, and they lean on me, which is exactly what a family should be about.

So, we will end this book in the same way that we started it, by restating something we have said dozens of times by now: *It is worth it*. Every cry, every scream, every temper tantrum, every argument, and every patient moment of instruction, will be worth it in the end. Even if you do not follow the guidelines in my book, and simply love your child as you know he or she needs, you will be fine. You do not need to print off the nine rules that we discussed a few chapters ago as if it is some kind of master playbook for life. Spend time with your child, seek to understand them, be patient with them, and everything else will fall in line.

Who knows? Maybe at some point in the future, you will be talking to somebody else who has a strong-willed child and they will ask you how you raised such a successful person. You can look them in the eye and tell them exactly what you did, but, most importantly, you will be able to tell them there is a light at the end of the tunnel—that there is hope. That is all they really need to hear anyway, and in reality, is all the strong-willed child needs to understand as well. There is hope.

We just have to hold onto it.

Epilogue: How to Parent a Strong-Willed Child During a Global Pandemic

When I originally set out to write this book, I never, for one second, imagined I would be speaking to an entire generation of people trying to parent strong-willed children in the middle of a global pandemic. Considering the fact that global pandemics only happen about once every 80 years or so, the fact that you're having to parent small children during that minuscule time is difficult enough, much less when you're dealing with one who tries to defy you every step.

And although the steps I outlined in the previous chapters are fine, I wanted to include something at the end specifically for "quarantine-based parenting." I understand full well that many states (and countries) are now lifting their lockdown restrictions—for better or for worse—but that doesn't mean this information won't apply in the future somehow. If there is a meningitis outbreak at your school, for instance, or some other kind of illness that shuts down your normal means of education or daycare, you'll be left with a child inside your house for an extended period of time, and one who yet still needs to maintain their normal routine.

When that happens, I would encourage you to re-consult this advice.

Admittedly, I am not the world's foremost expert on epidemiology, nor have I had decades of experience in this particular arena. Instead, I'm someone who's had to watch parents struggle to maintain a sense of normalcy in their child's topsy-turvy lives. Along the way, I've noticed a few key factors that play into whether a parent will be successful during this time or not. Below are a few of the main things that I've learned.

A Routine is More Important Than Ever

If you haven't developed some kind of day-to-day routine for your child, now is the time. When everything else in their life is going upside down, and they can't see their friends because of this or that reason, they need to have a sense of structure baked into their everyday lives to lean on.

This may consist of structured TV time, outdoor time, or school time, but your child functions best when they wake up in the morning and know exactly what they're going to do throughout the day, and more importantly, what is expected of them throughout the day.

This applies to the parent just as well as it does the child. Even though I am not self-employed, my job requires me to think as such, and I can attest to you the value of having a routine to function in everyday life. Even something as simple as waking up at the same time every day and answering emails only during a select few times can pay huge dividends for your mental health. If you can do that for you, why should it not work for your child?

The last thing you want is for your kid to have a blank canvas for the entire day, free to create it how they wish. You know what's best for them, and you know what needs to get done, so build it into their everyday routine. Learn to think like a homeschooling parent; whether you agree with that approach or not, they have the system down cold.

If I could give you one piece of advice to best survive this pandemic, having a routine would be it. While you can always add in the other ones later, without this central part, everything else will fall apart. Buy a whiteboard, get a calendar, set some sticky notes out—whatever you have to do, make sure that you stay organized.

Keep Your Sense of Humor

Most likely, unless your child has a weird interest in obscure bacteria and viruses, they won't understand why they can't go to class with their friends. Try as you might to explain it to them, you'll find yourself running into roadblock after roadblock, struggling to find the words that can help communicate it to them. A strong-willed child will fight even harder against this, not only asking to go to school, but in some cases, even demanding it (surprisingly). What are you supposed to do in those situations?

Keep a smile. Though the situation isn't ideal for anybody, look at this is an excellent opportunity for you to have some one-on-one time. Talk to them about the merits of getting their schoolwork done early so they can have the rest of the day to play. Plan an adventure for them, even if it's in your own backyard, so they have something to look forward to.

And please, for your own sanity's sake, try to keep the news turned off as much as possible. You don't want to be filling your head with negative issues of the day, while then trying to force a smile to keep your family's attitude positive. You'll only burn yourself out way earlier than you need to, and then be back at square one once you recover.

Be More Flexible Than Ever

As we stated in earlier chapters, the parent of a strong-willed child needs to be flexible. They'll have to bend to their child's wishes, acquiesce to the endless amount of questions, and also remain calm when it seems like everything is flying off the handle.

When you're in the middle of a quarantine, though, expect to take it up to an even higher level.

There are no answers that can satisfy why your child has to stay home all day, especially if they're used to going out all the time. And if you have a strong-willed teenager, this can get even more stressful, as social skills play into the personal development of a teenager so heavily.

To help with this, try to be more flexible in what you allow them to do. Let them stay up a little later than normal, play video games a little longer, or fix their favorite foods more often. It's not a pattern you want to keep going once things return to "normal," but it will provide a little less chaos in what can otherwise be a turbulent time.

Take Time for Yourself

As the quarantine goes on, you will begin to feel the walls start to close in on you. It can be a suffocating time, as the faces that surround you all day become the only faces you see at all. Without friends, without an outside life, without anything to take the stress from 24/7 parenting, it's not just a possibility you'll get overwhelmed, it's a virtual certainty.

Because of that, it's more important than ever that you take some time for yourself. Go read a book for a few hours, take up a hobby, or binge a little bit more on Netflix than you would normally. The same allowances you would give your child apply to you as well, but I would argue they are even more important for you than for them.

Some people will shrug this off, believing they are stronger than that and don't need time set aside. Those people will almost always doom themselves to failure, many times without even realizing it. Still others will feel guilty for taking time for themselves; after all, in a global pandemic, shouldn't this be the time they are more present than ever?

Quality over quantity. Make the moments you're with your children count, but don't be afraid to take some time for yourself. Just like when flying, put your mask on before helping others. In doing this, you both save yourself and those who are under your charge.

Remind Yourself It's Only Temporary.

I often encourage parents to think about the long term when it comes to parenting a strong-willed child, but when you're in the middle of a quarantine or confined in your home for any reason, you need to switch your thinking from years to days or even months in advance. Instead of thinking about what life will be like a decade from now, try reminding yourself the situation you're embroiled in is only temporary, and with any luck, will change sooner rather than later.

This isn't just for your own sanity; instead it's for perseverance's sake. You would never, in a million years, allow your child to have such an off-balanced view of the world, where more than usual is let slide and regular routines are slightly ignored—but you will for now. It's not just a good idea; in some cases, it's an imperative. The only thing that will allow you to have some measure of confidence in what you're doing is the understanding that it won't last forever.

Of course, a part of this is understanding when things do return to normal, it'll be a little bit more difficult to get them adapted to their old routine, but you can plan for that as it goes on. As it seems like the confinement is growing closer to an end, start to pull back on some of those allowances little by little so they don't react negatively at the beginning. Allow the return to normalcy to sink in over time, and you'll have a much easier go of it.

Global pandemics are tough for everyone involved, but don't let this be a time you just "muscle through"—make it an opportunity for you and your family to draw closer. Who knows, maybe you'll look back fondly at this time of your life and see it as the opportunity you needed to draw closer than ever before.

CPSIA information can be obtained
at www.ICGtesting.com
Printed in the USA
LVHW050616210223
739962LV00012B/600